Taking on Staff

Taking on Staff

Recruiting and retaining the best staff for your business

Erika Lucas

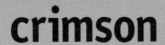

Taking on Staff: Recruiting and retaining the best staff for your business

This first edition published in 2013 by Crimson Publishing Ltd., Westminster House, Kew Road, Richmond, Surrey TW9 2ND

© Crimson Publishing 2013

Author: Erika Lucas

British Library Cataloguing in Publication Data
A catalogue record for this book is available from the British Library

ISBN 978 1 85458 673 5

Typeset by IDSUK (DataConnection) Ltd
Printed and bound in Great Britain by TJ International Ltd, Padstow, Cornwall

Contents

Contents

Introduction

I f you're reading this book it's likely you've already decided you need to hire – or you may have already taken the plunge and are now planning to take on more staff to help grow your business.

Employing people for the first time is undoubtedly a scary prospect for the small business owner. People are worried about whether the business can really afford it and if they will be able to keep enough work coming in to pay someone else's wages.

They are concerned that they will become embroiled in endless paperwork, bound up in bureaucracy, or that they might misunderstand some of the legislation and get it horribly wrong.

There's also a tendency for entrepreneurs in the early stages of building their business to feel that they have to do it all themselves – or that no one else could possibly do it as well as they can. They are anxious that staff may not represent the business professionally to customers; that employees won't take a conscientious approach to their work; or – worse – that they will steal the best ideas and run off with all the clients.

It's important to recognise, however, that if your business is going to grow, you can't possibly do everything yourself for ever. Yes, of course, in the early stages you may well be doing everything from answering the phone and packaging up products to negotiating deals with suppliers and handling the marketing. Indeed, there is an argument that being very hands-on at the beginning is valuable and that you need to know the fine detail of what's involved before you can start delegating tasks to someone else.

At some stage, however, you will need to let go of the reins a little and share the day-to-day workload, so that you can concentrate on developing your product or service and on bringing in new business.

The good news is that if you've made the decision that the time is right to hire staff, this book has everything you need to help you get it right.

↩ *CHAPTER 1*

To hire or not to hire

📖 What's in this chapter?

Taking on staff is a big commitment, and you'll need to ask yourself some important questions to make sure you are hiring for the right reasons.

In this chapter we'll cover:

→ how you know when it's the right time to hire

→ identifying the tipping point for your business – when it all gets too much and you can no longer cope without additional help

→ the key issues you need to think about before you launch in and advertise that vacancy

→ how you can make sure you are hiring for the right reasons.

Finding the right time

So how do you know when it's the appropriate time to hire someone? And how do you go about making sure you employ the right people who will represent your business well and help you grow?

In an ideal world, it's just before all the plates you've been balancing come crashing down around you and you let a client or customer down badly. In other words, the decision to recruit shouldn't really be made when you're in a crisis situation. If your back is up against the wall, you're much more likely to take someone on because they're immediately available, rather than because they're the right person for the job.

Identifying the tipping point

There's no magic formula to help you decide when it's the right time to recruit. The circumstances and the timing will be different for every business. The key, however, is to find the individual tipping point for your business.

It's about sitting back, taking a long hard look at what you do and how you do it and thinking carefully about exactly what difference employing someone will make.

If you can, it's good to think beyond your immediate needs and to look ahead.

A difficult and ever-changing economic climate makes long-term planning tricky, but hopefully you will have at least some idea of how you want the business to develop and where you would like to be in a year's time. In other words, the recruitment decisions you make should ideally both help you manage better today and also support your plans for tomorrow.

So think about recruitment against the backdrop of your business plan. What skills and experience does your company need if it is to grow? What can you realistically manage yourself with your current skill-set and where do you need additional expertise?

"It's vital to be strictly honest about your strengths and weaknesses," says Berkshire-based business adviser Brian Steel. "And it should be an ongoing process. Continuous improvement comes through continuous monitoring."

Key questions to ask

Try asking yourself the following questions.

- Are you thinking about taking on more people to help you *grow* your business or because you can no longer manage the workload yourself?
- If you are struggling with an increased workload, is it a temporary issue (eg caused by a seasonal influx or a large-scale project) or is it likely to be a long-term trend?
- Do you need more people – or do you need to do things differently? Could you make better use of technology, for example, to get tasks done more quickly and efficiently? Could you find ways to streamline some of your processes to cut down on unnecessary admin?
- Do you need people to bring new skills and expertise into the business to complement your own? If so, are you clear about what these skills are and exactly how they will help your business grow?
- Do you need someone to take over a particular area or set of tasks (eg book-keeping or marketing)? Is there enough work to do in these areas to justify a permanent employee, or might outsourcing to a specialist be a better solution?
- Are you considering hiring because there are areas of the business where you feel out of your comfort zone (sales or finance, for instance)? Is recruitment the right answer – or do you need to learn how to do these things yourself?
- What are the practical implications of taking someone on? Where will they work from, for example? Do you have room to accommodate them and have you taken into account the financial implications of possibly having to buy new equipment or furniture?
- Is there anything you need to stop doing? Are you in danger, for example, of taking people on to maintain a line of work which is time-consuming but actually not very profitable?
- What will happen if you don't hire anyone? Is maintaining the status quo a viable option?

These questions should help you weigh up whether it's the right time to recruit, and will give you a clearer picture of what the implications of taking staff on will be.

Hiring for the right reasons

It is really important to make sure you are hiring for the right reasons. Don't fall into the trap of taking someone on because it makes you feel important, because you think it makes the business look more credible or because you've met someone you know would do a great job.

Of course, if you are still unsure, you can also seek advice from the professionals. Your bank manager or accountant will be happy, for instance, to talk through the financial implications of employing someone (salary, sick pay, insurance costs, additional equipment, etc) and give their guidance on whether they think your business can stand it. If you have access to the services of a business adviser or coach, they can help you think through the pros and cons of dipping your toe in the recruitment waters.

You will probably find that the experts fall into one of two camps. Some will take the view that you shouldn't sweat the small stuff, and should hire people in to do those things that are taking up valuable time and head space and holding you back.

Others argue that you should only hire when you start to feel the pain – or put another way, when there is more work than you can possibly cope with and you can see it's going to be that way for the foreseeable future.

In their book *ReWork: Change the Way You Work Forever* (Vermillion, March 2010), Jason Fried and David Heinemeier Hansson suggest a different take on hiring.

> *If you feel like you're not coping you can either hire your way out of it or you can learn your way out of it. Try learning first. What you give up in initial execution will be repaid many times over by the wisdom you gain. Plus, you should want to be intimately involved in all aspects of your business. Otherwise you'll wind up in the dark, putting your fate solely in the hands of others. That's dangerous.*

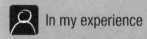

In my experience

Claire Pedrick, 3D Coaching

The right time to hire is "just before you need to do it", according to Claire Pedrick, Managing Director of 3D Coaching.

Sheer pressure of work prompted Claire to take on her first employee – an administrator who could ease the day-to-day paperwork burden.

This freed up almost a third of her time and allowed her to concentrate on client work. But as demand from clients continued to grow, Claire found herself facing something of a dilemma.

3D already worked with a team of associates, who were brought in on an ad hoc basis to meet the needs of individual and corporate clients. But Claire recognised that however good they were, these associates would always put the needs of their own businesses first.

"What I really needed was people who would actually help grow the business as well as deliver my products and services," she explains. "There were two people who were great and I really wanted to work with them, but they were effectively working in competition with me.

"The big question for me was what was going to be the difference between an associate and an employee – and the answer was that the pay-off is loyalty. I knew if I said come in and be an employee they would be 100% loyal and would help me expand.

"We sat down and really considered how it would work. I set up a share scheme so that they could share both the risk and the reward – and both of them have brought in their own work from the beginning. Now that I look back it has been a real catalyst. I started out as a sole trader and now I have an organisation where a lot of our customers have absolutely no idea who I am and that for me is a big win."

Checklist

☑ Find the tipping point for your business. Assess where your time is being spent and whether there are solutions to make processes more efficient.

☑ Look at your rate of growth over a sustained period and try to project how things are likely to develop in the next year.

☑ Consider your financial position and whether an extra salary will eat into your profit or help you grow the business and profits sufficiently to absorb the cost.

☑ Look at your own position and role in hiring. Will the recruit need to be trained and managed? How will that affect your ability to deliver? Will delegating certain tasks free you up to bring in more business?

CHAPTER 2

Considering the employment options

📖 What's in this chapter?

There are many options for employing people, and you need to make sure you choose the right one for your business. You'll need to understand the pros and cons of the different approaches, and be able to answer some key questions.

In this chapter we'll look at these questions.

→ Is a permanent employee the right choice for your business?

→ How do fixed term contracts work?

→ What are the advantages of a zero hours contract?

→ Is taking on temporary staff a good way to test the waters?

→ What are the pros and cons of using freelancers, consultants or contractors?

Once you've made the decision to hire, look carefully at the different employment options open to you.

There's a tendency for businesses to think that hiring someone means taking on a full-time, permanent employee. That's a big commitment – and, quite frankly, for many people it's quite a daunting prospect.

But a conventional full-time contract isn't the only option. There are a number of ways you can employ people, depending on what best suits your business and your circumstances.

Monday to Friday, 9 to 5 may work well, for example, if you run an office-based business where customers and clients expect to be able to contact you during normal weekday working hours.

A retail business, however, might be open long hours, seven days a week, and would probably need a team of part-timers working a variety of hours to cover late nights and weekends.

Some industries, such as the media, typically find their need for staff fluctuates depending on the ebb and flow of projects that come in. Other businesses, such as tourism, may experience seasonal peaks and troughs.

It's important to be really clear about exactly when and how often you need people to be working for you before you make the decision about which employment option to go for. Otherwise, you may find yourself struggling to cope with a heavy workload with too few people – or with employees who are sitting around twiddling their thumbs because there isn't enough for them to do.

Key questions to ask

Try asking yourself the following questions.

- How many hours do I need someone to work each week?
- Will I need that number of hours all the time – or only some of the time?
- Am I sure there will be enough work to keep a new employee fully occupied during those hours?

- Is the workload likely to vary enormously – or only slightly – from week to week?
- Are there likely to be seasonal peaks and troughs? If so, when are the key times?
- Can one full-time person meet my needs – or would I be better off with a combination of people working under different arrangements (full-time, part-time, temporary, etc)?

These questions may seem obvious, but it's surprising how many businesses rush into contractual arrangements that don't actually meet their needs. A bit of careful thought at this early stage can save a lot of time, money and angst in the long run.

The following are the employment options that are available, depending on your needs.

Permanent employees

A permanent employee can be full-time or part-time. They have an ongoing employment contract with you and you have to fulfil a range of obligations to them (paid holiday, sick pay, etc) depending on how long they have been with you and on the terms of the contract you enter into with them (more about this in Chapter 8).

-> **The pros:** predictability, regularity, loyalty, potential.

-> **The cons:** management time, full range of legal obligations, lack of flexibility.

Fixed-term contract employees

A fixed-term contract employee has a contract with you, but only for a set time (such as six months) or until a specific task or project has been completed. They have the same employment rights as a permanent member of staff – but your obligations to them only last for the duration of the contract. This can work well in a number of scenarios. You may want to take someone on to cover a seasonal peak (in the retail or leisure industry for instance). A party planner might need an extra pair of hands for just a few months in the lead-up to a big event. Or a consultant may need to take on extra resources to deliver a big project on time.

➯ **The pros:** predictability, extra resource only when you need it.

➯ **The cons:** management time, full range of legal obligations.

Zero hours contract employees

A zero hours contract means you can effectively have people "on call" to work when you need them. It's important to recognise, however, that this is not a one-way street. You are not obliged to provide these employees with work – but, equally, they are not obliged to accept the work if it doesn't suit them at the time.

Your obligations as an employer will depend on the kind of contract you draw up (more about this in Chapter 8). This kind of arrangement can work well in industries such as the media, for example, where work can be unpredictable and skilled staff are often needed for sustained periods at short notice.

➯ **The pros:** flexibility, limited employer obligations, cost-effective.

➯ **The cons:** lack of loyalty, unpredictable resources.

Temporary agency staff

Many fledgling businesses choose to dip their toe in the recruitment waters by using temporary staff supplied by an employment agency. This is a low-risk way of trying people out and getting a clear idea of the amount of time/resources you need – but it is of course a more expensive option than employing someone directly as you will be paying agency fees and commission.

Typically, your contract is with the agency, which will pay the individual and deal with issues such as National Insurance Contributions (NICs). You do, however, still have certain legal responsibilities towards temporary staff – providing a safe working environment and appropriate rest breaks, for example.

Bear in mind that legislation which came into force in October 2011 means that agency workers will be entitled to the same basic pay and benefits as permanent employees after 12 weeks in an assignment (Agency Workers Regulations).

-> **The pros:** flexible, available at short notice, limited employer obligations.

-> **The cons:** more expensive, quality of people may vary, lack of commitment/loyalty.

Freelancers, consultants and contractors

Many businesses decide to fill their resource needs by bringing in freelancers, consultants or contractors. A building company, for example, might call on a range of contractors with specific skills (plumbing, carpentry, etc) to help them complete a new build or refurbishment. Publishing is an industry where freelance writers, editors and designers are often brought in to work on specific projects or to meet tight deadlines. Professional services firms or small consultancies often call in other consultants, whose skills are complementary to their own, to help meet client needs.

This is not an employment relationship, but it is relevant in this context as it can help you decide what needs your business has. The freelancer or consultant is self-employed, selling their services to you, and your legal obligations are minimal. If you go down this route, however, it's important to make sure that the individual concerned is legally defined as self-employed.

It's a complex area. Her Majesty's Revenue and Customs (HMRC) suggests that the best way to define someone's employment status is to ask the following key questions.

If the answer to all the following questions is "Yes", the worker is probably an employee.

-↷ Do they have to do the work themselves?

-↷ Can someone tell them at any time what to do, where to carry out the work or when and how to do it?

-↷ Can they work a set amount of hours?

-↷ Can someone move them from task to task?

-↷ Are they paid by the hour, week or month?

-↷ Can they get overtime pay or bonus payment?

If the answer to all the following questions is "Yes", it will usually mean that the worker is self-employed.

-↷ Can they hire someone to do the work or engage helpers at their own expense?

-↷ Do they risk their own money?

-↷ Do they provide the main items of equipment they need to do their job, not just the small tools that many employees provide for themselves?

-↷ Do they agree to do a job for a fixed price regardless of how long the job may take?

-↷ Can they decide what work to do, how and when to do the work and where to provide the services?

-↷ Do they regularly work for a number of different people?

-↷ Do they have to correct unsatisfactory work in their own time and at their own expense?

It's important to satisfy yourself about a freelancer's circumstances before you engage their services. You may find yourself on dodgy ground, for instance, if a freelancer is working a significant amount of hours, only for you, over a sustained period. If this is the case, they could in effect be considered to be in an employment relationship with you.

If you are unsure, HMRC's guide *Employment Status: Employed or Self Employed?* is available online to give further guidance. There's also an online employment status indicator you can use to help you decide (www.hmrc.gov.uk/calcs/esi.htm).

It's important to recognise that it is *your* responsibility to establish the correct employment status of someone who works for you. Ignorance will not be regarded as an excuse.

There are special rules about employing contractors for the construction industry. Full details of these can be found on the HMRC website (www.hmrc.gov.uk/cis/contractors/advice-pay.htm).

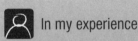 In my experience

Claudia Boroughs, Beautiful You

When Claudia Boroughs set up her salon Beautiful You she thought long and hard about what kind of staff support she would need.

She recognised that it would be difficult to satisfy customer demand and grow the business if she were the sole therapist. There was also the issue of who would answer the phone, greet clients and book appointments when she was behind closed doors in one of the treatment rooms.

"My mum had offered to help me out and cover the reception part-time, but it meant there was still going to be a lot of time when I was on my own, and I could see it just wouldn't work," she explained. "It would be difficult to give people appointments at the time they wanted them, or to provide the kind of atmosphere and level of customer service I had in mind for the salon."

It's quite common in the beauty industry to have therapists working on a self-employed basis or renting space in a salon in return for a fee or percentage on treatments. Claudia felt, however, that as a fledgling business she needed another permanent therapist who would work full-time and help build long-lasting relationships with clients.

A therapist she had previously worked with had just returned from travelling and agreed to join her on a permanent, full-time contract. Claudia admits to having a few nervous moments about whether it would be possible to pull clients in quickly enough to sustain two therapists working full-time.

"It was a bit of a gamble but I really didn't want to have to turn people away – or to have to worry about a self-employed person up and leaving, taking clients with them. I had worked with the therapist I took on before, so I knew she was good at her job and that people liked her, so although it was a risk, I felt it was the only way I would be able to grow the business."

The gamble paid off. An introductory discount kept new clients pouring in and the salon was booked solid for the first few months. Business has continued to grow and Claudia has since taken on a part-timer on a permanent contract with a minimum number of guaranteed hours. A self-employed therapist also provides additional support at busy times.

Claudia hopes that if business continues to be good, she will be able to take on another full-time therapist within a year.

 Checklist

☑ Think carefully about exactly when and how often you need people to work for you.

☑ Make sure you have a clear idea of the work that needs to be done and whether it needs a full- or part-time person.

☑ Gen up on the range of employment options available to you.

☑ Consider the pros and cons of each option and work out which will work best for your business.

☑ Check the status of freelance or contract staff to make sure HMRC would consider them self-employed.

☑ If you are planning to use agency workers, make sure you are up to date on recent changes to the legislation.

☑ Don't fall foul of the law. If in doubt, seek advice from the experts. A human resources (HR) consultant or employment lawyer will be able to advise you.

↶ *CHAPTER 3*
Employing young people

📖 What's in this chapter?

Employing an experienced candidate is not always the best or only option. Young people can offer a range of talents, and can be a great asset to your business.

In this chapter we'll look at these questions.

→ Is taking on an apprentice the right move for your business and how do you go about finding one?

→ What are the advantages of taking on an intern for a short-term placement?

→ Should you pay them, and if so, how much?

→ How can a work placement student help you, and what do you need to do to get the most out of the time they spend with you?

→ Why is it worth seriously considering requests from schools for work experience placements?

W e've all read the headlines about the depressing number of young people coming out of school and university with no jobs to go to. There's a huge market of untapped potential out there, which small businesses are largely missing out on.

If you're only just starting to dip your toe in the recruitment waters, it's easy to come to the conclusion that a seasoned candidate will always be your best option. You may feel you don't have time to nurture an inexperienced employee, or that you will struggle to find the funds to invest in their training.

There are many occasions when you need someone who can hit the ground running. But there are also many scenarios when employing someone at the start of their career could bring enormous benefits to your business. A small amount of time and investment up front can pay big dividends later and might even help you steal a march on the competition.

A young recruit may not have hands-on experience, but they are likely to bring enthusiasm and a new perspective. Best of all, you have the opportunity to grow them alongside your business, and to develop their talents in a way that suits your company's specific needs.

This chapter will help you weigh up some of the options for employing young people and decide whether it's a suitable route for you.

Apprenticeships

If you hear the word "apprentice", you will probably immediately think of one of the hands-on professions such as plumbing or engineering (or maybe of Lord Sugar grilling his latest unfortunate victim in the boardroom!).

It's a misconception, however, that apprenticeships are just for the manual trades. They are in fact available in over 200 professions, ranging from accountancy, IT and business administration to veterinary nursing, hospitality and floristry.

Small businesses are often concerned that taking on an apprentice will be just too much hassle. They are worried they will get bound up in excessive paperwork and that it will take too long before a young recruit will be able to add any real value to the business.

The reality, however, is that investing in an apprenticeship can pay real dividends. It's a great way to bring the skills you will need for the future into the business and to ensure that new recruits are trained in your mould and to meet your needs.

A well-developed and supported young person can bring enthusiasm, commitment and a fresh perspective to the job. They will also be able to provide you with a valuable insight into how their generation communicates and might want to engage with your business in the future.

Taking on an apprentice really shouldn't be time-consuming or difficult once you've put in place the basic foundations to manage them, and there is plenty of support and advice from the National Apprenticeship Service (NAS) (www.apprenticeships.org.uk) to help you get up and running.

The NAS has a team of advisers who can help you decide whether taking on an apprentice is right for you. They will also support you throughout the process, from getting the paperwork in order to putting you in touch with an appropriate training provider.

Your training provider will also work closely with you to manage the training, making sure that the learning both on and off the job is integrated, relevant to your business and completed to the required standard.

Facts, figures and food for thought . . .

Researchers have attempted to pin down the financial benefits of apprenticeships. A 2007 study by Sheffield University found that a Level 3 advanced apprentice (see p. 20) will generate an additional lifetime benefit to themselves and their employer of £105,000 compared to someone who does not gain an Apprenticeship. The additional benefit for someone who studies up to Level 2 is £73,000.

How does it work?

Apprenticeships are officially described as "work-based training programmes designed around the needs of employers, which lead to national recognised qualifications".

What that means in practice is that you employ an apprentice and they work and learn on the job, backed up by regular training either at their local college or with a specialist training provider. An apprentice plumber, for example, would typically spend four days a week out on the job and one day a week at college.

All the training that takes place, both on and off the job, is geared towards achieving a National Vocational Qualification (NVQ) or other appropriate certificate. The training provider works closely with you to monitor and manage their learning. Apprenticeships are open to candidates aged 16 and over who can be either new recruits to your business or existing employees.

Different types of apprenticeship

There are three levels of apprenticeship.

1. **Intermediate level.** The intermediate level provides the basic skills an apprentice needs for their chosen career. It usually leads to an NVQ Level 2 and in most cases a relevant knowledge-based qualification, such as a BTEC. Apprentices who successfully complete the intermediate level can move onto the advanced level apprenticeship.

2. **Advanced level.** The advanced level leads to an NVQ Level 3 and in most cases a BTEC or similar certificate. To start at advanced level, a candidate should ideally have five GCSEs at grade C or above or have completed the intermediate level apprenticeship.

3. **Higher level.** Apprentices taking the higher-level route work towards work-based learning qualifications such as an NVQ Level 4 and, in some cases, a knowledge-based qualification such as a Foundation degree.

There's an expectation that an apprentice will be either working or learning for a minimum of 30 hours per week, although part-time apprenticeships are available in a limited number of cases.

What does it cost?

The national minimum wage for apprentices, at the time of writing, is £2.65 per hour, although in practice most employers pay more than this. If your apprentice is over the age of 19, they are entitled to the national minimum wage rate for their age (see p. 53).

You would certainly want to think about increasing the hourly rate you pay as the trainee starts to build their skills, although it is up to you to decide what is appropriate and what you can afford. The average net pay for an apprentice is in fact £170 per week.

Apprentices have to be paid for the time they are learning – ie the time they spend at college or with a training provider – as well as for the time they are working.

Who pays for the training?

The training the apprentice does at college or with a specialist training provider is paid for either in full or in part by the NAS.

For apprentices aged 16–18, the full cost of the training is funded. For those aged 19 and over, it is subsidised by half. The funding goes directly to the college or training provider – not to the employer.

Finding an apprentice

If you are in an industry where apprenticeships are common, you will probably be inundated with letters from young people seeking placements. If you need to find a candidate, however, there is an online matching system – Apprenticeship Vacancies – to help you find the right person quickly and easily.

You simply supply details of the opportunity and the system matches it with suitable candidates who have registered an interest in finding a placement. Potential recruits are sent an email inviting them to apply, and you are then sent a list of possible candidates to shortlist and interview.

You need to pay the same attention to recruiting an apprentice as you would any other employee, so make sure that there will be enough work for them to do and that you find a candidate who has both the aptitude and enthusiasm for the job.

It's not just for big business . . .

Apprenticeships are not just for the big players. There are many small businesses that are building their operations by successfully "growing their own".

- → Essex-based telecoms company Polaris has taken on an IT apprentice to help redevelop the company's website and make the most of social media platforms such as LinkedIn, Facebook and Twitter.

- → Lincoln-based Forum Computers has built a team of seven staff, all of whom are under 25 and have developed into fully fledged technicians via the apprenticeship route.

- → Bridlington-based Fish and Chips at 149 was set up two years ago and now counts five apprentices among its team of 10 staff. It has won an industry award for best UK fish and chip restaurant and has also been shortlisted in the small employer of the year category in the 2011 National Apprenticeship Awards.

- → Mark Brown, owner of Manchester-based Editors Keys, took on a business administration apprentice to support the growth of his company — a supplier of specialist editing keyboards for the TV and audio industry. "Like many other business owners I had my reservations about employing an apprentice, but it's been one of the best decisions for our company since we started," he says. "It's allowed us to get that extra help we needed as well as help to develop and train an enthusiastic new member of staff."

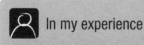 **In my experience**

John and Gaynor McNally, Greenfields Kennels and Cattery

When John and Gaynor McNally bought Greenfields Kennels and Cattery six years ago, the business was run down and in great need of updating and improving. The couple had three members of staff – two full-time and one apprentice. They were new to the apprenticeship programme and didn't know how it would work. They knew that it wasn't just the bricks and mortar that needed to change, but also the staffing and leadership. As they built the business, John and Gaynor realised the importance of employing young people who are keen, committed and eager to learn.

When the apprentices sign up they have very little idea of what it takes to be a kennel officer, which is a very responsible job. They are not thrown in at the deep end when they arrive, but are guided through their work step by step to ensure that they are confident with each role before moving on to the next. Initially they work alongside a very experienced member of staff who will monitor them at all times, and as they progress, they are regularly examined to ensure that all policies and procedures are followed. They are encouraged to ask questions, no matter how trivial they may seem.

Apprentices attend Reaseheath College one day a week, where they work towards gaining an NVQ2 in Animal Care. John and Gaynor are committed to helping them achieve their NVQ, and will give whatever help and guidance is required, including helping with college work in the evenings. One mother of an apprentice wrote to the couple to say how much her daughter had matured since starting at Greenfields, and she was convinced it was because she was so happy in her work.

John and Gaynor have worked hard to create confident and pleasant adults who have a strong belief in the importance of commitment, hard work and teamwork. This has been a huge success, with customers frequently commenting on the pleasant, caring staff. In return, the apprentices have brought energy and vitality to Greenfield, and with their help they have built up the daily average intake from 24 to 118 dogs and from 16 to 40 cats. This has resulted in increased profits for the kennels and cattery, which has enabled the business to improve and expand. With the support of Reaseheath College, apprentices have gone on to become managers and mentors.

Courtesy of www.apprenticeships.org.uk.

Internships

Internships have received a lot of publicity lately, and not all of it has been good. There has been much public debate about graduates being exploited by employers who are reportedly using a rolling programme of unpaid placements as an alternative to taking on a salaried employee.

There have also been reports of internships at top city firms being "auctioned off" to the highest bidder and of young people being expected to work long hours without even their food and travel expenses being covered.

The lines between unpaid work experience and paid work placements have become increasingly blurred, and the government is under pressure to take action against unscrupulous employers who flout the rules to their advantage.

Managed well, however, an internship is a win–win situation, and it can certainly be a viable option for a small business. The business gets an extra pair of hands to fulfil a short-term resourcing need or to take on a particular project that keeps getting put on the back burner because no one has time to do it in addition to their "day job".

It's also a great way for a small business to get new ideas, gain a fresh perspective and to bring in skills it currently doesn't have – knowledge of how to exploit some of the latest technology, for example. An internship can also help a business identify possible future candidates who can help grow the company and eventually take on a permanent role.

In return, the graduate gets some solid work experience to put on their CV, as well as the chance to develop knowledge of their chosen profession and to make some valuable contacts in their sector. They also get the opportunity to improve their future employability by developing their skills in key areas such as commercial awareness, communication and customer service.

How it works

An internship is typically a work placement that lasts between three and 12 months, depending on the circumstances of the individual and the business. It's an opportunity that is most commonly sought after by graduates who have finished their university or college course and are looking for some experience that will help give them a leg up into their chosen profession.

There is an ongoing debate around the issue of whether interns should be paid, and it is a bit of a grey area. It's perfectly legal to employ an intern without paying them – although in practice, most organisations do provide some level of compensation.

You wouldn't expect to pay an intern the same salary as a full-time, experienced employee. They are, after all, new to the world of work and will need help and support to develop their skills. But they do add value to the workforce and can quite quickly become productive employees – and there is a growing body of opinion that they should be paid at least a "training wage" in the same way as an apprentice.

A recent survey from the Chartered Institute of Personnel and Development (CIPD) (Learning and Talent Development Survey, 2010) suggested that 63% of companies pay interns at least the national minimum wage (NMW), with 92% choosing to pay more than the going rate. It's also common for interns to be reimbursed for their travel and subsistence expenses.

Some organisations, however, class their interns as volunteers with no kind of contract or formal arrangement, in which case the NMW rules don't apply.

> ✐ **Startups Tip**
>
> Follow the CIPD's advice to help you decide whether your intern should be paid:
>
> "If an intern is contributing to your company, has a list of duties and is working set hours then technically they should be paid the National Minimum Wage."

Ethics aside, there is of course also an argument to say that an intern who is being paid will feel much more valued by the business and is more likely to approach their placement with energy and enthusiasm.

Don't forget that if you are paying an intern, you will need to add them to your payroll system so that they receive their salary and expenses at the end of each month in the usual way.

Even though an internship is not a formal contractual arrangement, you still have the same duty of care towards an intern as any other member of staff, and you should treat them with respect and consideration and ensure their health and safety.

Some businesses do issue voluntary internship agreements – a great way to demonstrate your commitment to providing a professionally managed placement and to make sure both parties' expectations are clear from the outset.

The CIPD provides a sample internship agreement (see the opposite page), although you can draw up your own.

Internship agreement

To be read carefully and signed by the intern and the employer (please make two copies).

The Employer's Responsibilities

As the employer, I am aware that interns provide a useful service for our company. I confirm that I will abide by the principles outlined in the CIPD *Employer's Guide to Internships* (a copy of which will be given to the intern) and it is therefore my responsibility to ensure that the intern will be:

- treated with respect at all times
- supported and trained appropriately for the tasks that they are asked to complete
- given as much access to learning and development opportunities as possible.

The Intern's Responsibilities

As an intern, I appreciate the opportunity that has been provided for me through this internship and understand that it offers the chance to gain experience and display professional development. Therefore I confirm that my responsibilities are to:

- behave in a professional manner at all times
- abide by the rules and regulations of this company
- work hard and diligently throughout the internship
- complete the projects and assignments given to me in a timely and accurate manner.

EMPLOYER   **INTERN**
Print Name   Print Name
Sign   Sign
Date   Date
Courtesy of CIPD

Finding an intern

You can recruit an intern in the same way you would recruit for any other vacancy – by placing an advertisement to invite applications, shortlisting candidates and conducting interviews (see Chapter 5).

There is also a web-based matching system, called Graduate Talent Pool, that can help you to find the right person (http://graduatetalentpool.bis.gov.uk).

You simply register on the website and fill in an online form with details of your vacancy, including a description of the role, the type of candidate you're looking for, the length of the internship and whether it is paid or unpaid.

To help screen candidates beforehand, you can also set up a list of 10 key questions applicants must answer correctly before they can get access to details of your opportunity.

Graduates who have registered on the website are able to search for suitable vacancies and can also sign up for email alerts which let them know when a relevant new opportunity is added.

Interested candidates contact you directly via whichever method you have specified (phone, email, CV, etc), and once you've received an application you just handle the interviewing and recruitment process in the usual way.

Making the most of an internship

If you're going to get the best out of an intern and provide them with a good experience, you need to spend some time up front thinking about how you are going to organise and manage the placement.

The following are some of the key issues to consider.

Induction
An intern will need an induction to your business in the same way as any other employee. In fact, if the placement is short, it's even more

important that they are given the information they need to hit the ground running. Make sure you introduce them to key members of staff and give them the background to your business and how they fit in. You also need to make sure they are familiar with your office practices and in particular with your health and safety policy. (There's more about induction processes in Chapter 11.)

Role and responsibilities

Interns need to be clear about exactly what they are expected to do. If you are charging them with a particular project, it's a good idea to draw up a project plan with milestones and regular opportunities to review progress. If you are planning on involving them across the business, it's good to think about what they will be doing, when and for who. You can do this on a week-by-week or month-by-month basis, depending on what suits your needs.

Learning opportunities

When you are putting a work or project plan together, remember that the aim is for the intern to learn as much as possible about your particular profession and what makes it tick. Think carefully about how you can expose them to opportunities that will genuinely help them develop their skills. Interns need to do their fair share of the tea-making and filing (or whatever the equivalent is in your business), but it is a waste of a placement to treat them like a dogsbody and restrict them purely to the menial tasks that no one else wants to do.

Management and support

It's important to recognise that interns may have had very little experience of the world of work and they will need support and supervision. Make sure you don't set them up for failure by assuming they will know how to approach tasks or to manage the day-to-day realities of work that come as second nature to you. You (or one of your team) will need to plan for investing a reasonable amount of time in briefing your intern fully and making sure they know how to carry out the tasks you are asking of them. Certainly in the early days they will need close management, regular feedback and supportive mentoring to help them deliver their best. The more you put in, the more you will get out.

Closing the placement

The end of a placement is a great opportunity to review progress and help the intern analyse what they've learned and how it might help them in their future career. Make sure you take the opportunity to conduct a full end of placement performance review and to provide the intern with a reference – unless you've decided to take them on yourself!

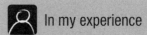

In my experience

Tina Webb at Tri-Synergy

Tri-Synergy Ltd is a marketing and business development company based in Hampshire. It specialises in marketing, internet marketing and PR.

The challenge

Managing Director Tina Webb explains:

"The qualities and skills of the people working for us are absolutely fundamental to the success of the company. We implemented a work experience scheme to combine the practical experience of the workforce in the company with fresh, innovative ideas brought in by the placement student.

"The benefit is threefold; we want our students to enjoy their placement and to learn both job skills and life skills, therefore we endeavour to add real 'value' for the student. The existing workforce learn the latest techniques within the internet marketing discipline and, last, the combination of both of these ensure that we have satisfied clients every time."

Placement benefits

- "New ideas into the organisation.
- The regular shake-up of the dynamics of our small business when a new person joins.
- Cost-effective method of bringing the latest knowledge and technology to the business."

Results

"Our placement students have bought real value to the organisation with innovative and fresh ideas, techniques and skills. Examples of tangible business benefits include:

- increased Tri-Synergy's product/service offering
- developed a new training manual used with all employees
- significantly increased clients' businesses and hence secured the client on an ongoing basis for the company."

Information provided by the National Council for Work Experience (NCWE)

Work placements

Sandwich and project placements

Young people who are in the midst of their studies are always looking for opportunities to gain solid work experience, and this is a great chance for your business to benefit from their intelligence and enthusiasm.

Small businesses often feel that taking someone on a work experience placement will be a lot of hassle for little reward, but there are plenty of examples of companies who have benefited enormously from hosting students on short-term project or longer-term sandwich placements. It's a great way to get an extra pair of hands to kick-start projects that have been sitting on the back burner, to investigate new markets or test the viability of new product ideas.

Research has shown that graduates themselves are becoming increasingly keen to work in small and start-up businesses. So why not take the opportunity to get your hands on some first-class graduate talent which might previously have only been available to the large corporates?

You can find students for these kind of placements via the Step programme, which is designed to help small businesses recruit

"work-ready" students to help with specific projects (www.step.org.
uk/default_employers.aspx). Step runs three programmes.

1. **Step Classic:** helps match employers with science, technology
    and engineering undergraduates looking for
    8–12-week project-based placements in the summer vacation.

2. **Graduate Step:** a programme designed to place recent graduates
    with employers for a 2–3 month period of "meaningful" work

3. **Step into Industry:** specialises in 6–12 month placements for
    undergraduates on their sandwich year (usually the period
    between their second and final year at university).

Step will help you develop a specification for your placement and
will promote the opportunity to its database of more than 20,000
students. It will provide a shortlist of pre-screened candidates, and
will support both yourself and the student over the course of
the placement.

As with any other kind of placement, you will need to invest time in
putting together a proper brief and supporting the student. However,
it's important to remember that these students have generally got
at least two years of their course behind them and will be able to
bring you specialist knowledge at a fraction of the cost a professional
service provider would charge.

You will be expected to compensate the student for their time, but
as you are not employing them there will be no employer National
Insurance (NI) or tax contributions to pay. At the time of writing, the
total cost of arranging a placement through Step is £315 per week. £217
of this is a training allowance which is paid to the student, with the
remainder going to Step to cover their management/administration of
the placement.

Step publishes a guide with advice for small businesses who may be
considering a graduate placement – *Managing Student and Graduate
Work Placements: A guide for employers* (www.step.org.uk/70332_SE_
Business.pdf). You can also email them at employers@step.org.uk or
phone them on 0844 2488 242.

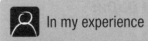 In my experience

Katherine Howell at Ultimate Salon

The Ultimate Salon was formed in 2002 and offers hair, beauty and tanning services in Nottingham's city centre. The salon was lacking a corporate image and did not have a defined marketing strategy, resulting in it missing the opportunity to capitalise on seasonal events such as Valentine's Day and Christmas.

With these problems in mind, Katherine Howell, studying Business Studies (Marketing) at Nottingham Trent University, was taken on.

To overcome the weak company identity and to reflect the salon's professional team, Katherine designed a range of business stationery, leaflets and posters. She also compiled an annual promotions schedule with accompanying promotional communications. To top it all off, she negotiated an array of advertising in local magazines and radio stations, while sticking to a very tight budget.

Karen Lamb was impressed with Katherine's professional nature, commitment and ability to work using her own initiative, was overwhelmed with the quality of her work and with the amount she achieved in the eight-week placement. When commenting on the benefits to Ultimate Salon, Karen Lamb stated, "Katherine's work has given us a vision and mission moving forward. We have professional packages including a corporate package which goes out to large local companies. Having professional literature has given us an edge over the competition in the local vicinity."

As a result of this experience, Karen Lamb strongly endorses the use of undergraduates and graduates within any business environment.

From *Managing Student and Graduate Work Placements: A guide for employers.*

(www.step.org.uk/70332_SE_Business.pdf)

Work experience for school pupils

If you're up and running as a small business you've undoubtedly already been asked at some stage to provide a work experience placement for a year 10 or 11 school pupil.

These are generally just week-long work placements designed to give pupils their first taste of working life and an idea of what kind of job they might or might not want to do.

When you're under pressure – as most small businesses are – it's easy to dismiss these requests out of hand as something you just don't have time for. Building links with your local school can, however, pay dividends in the long run. It's a great way to give back to your local community and to start to make contact with young people who may become valuable employees in the future.

Karen Moule, of marketing consultancy Enterprise Marketing, regularly hosts young people on work experience placements. She says that in her experience, the 16–18-year-olds who spend a week with her generally have "gritty determination, an entrepreneurial mindset, enthusiasm and a can-do attitude". Her business is just about to offer an administration apprenticeship to one such candidate who came on work experience and "never stopped asking questions the whole time he was here".

 Checklist

☑ Think carefully about whether a young person might meet your recruitment needs.

☑ Consider whether they could bring skills and talents to your business that you don't currently possess (knowledge of new technologies, for example).

☑ Gen up on the wide range of apprenticeships on offer and assess whether it's an approach that might work for your business.

☑ Think about projects you have on the back burner and assess whether an intern might be able to help you move them forward.

☑ Adopt a positive stance towards requests for work placements and consider how these might benefit your business in the long run.

 **CHAPTER 4**

Employing disabled people

📖 What's in this chapter?

Building a diverse workforce can offer benefits to your organisation, with disabled employees bringing valuable skills, talents and insights into your business.

In this chapter we'll cover:

→ the kind of adjustments you will have to make to your workplace if you employ a disabled person

→ what happens if someone you already employ becomes disabled

→ how to make sure your recruitment processes do not inadvertently discriminate against disabled people

→ what your legal obligations are when it comes to employing disabled people.

There's a tendency to assume that employing a disabled person will be "difficult", expensive and time-consuming. Businesses are concerned that they will have to make expensive adjustments to their workplace, that a disabled person is likely to take a lot of time off sick, or that they will need more support and supervision than other employees.

None of these things is necessarily true – and businesses who take this narrow view are missing out on a huge pool of talented employees who could be helping them build their business.

The facts speak for themselves. Over a third of businesses are struggling to find people with the right skills to fill their vacancies – yet 3.4 million disabled people are out of work. Those who are in employment are often in jobs where their skills are vastly under-utilised. Research suggests that at least 1.5 million part-time disabled workers are operating below their potential.

Taking a positive attitude to employing disabled people can bring a business many advantages.

→ It will give you a wider pool of candidates to choose from when you have a role to fill.

→ It can help to "future proof" your business. As the UK's population ages, the incidence of disability among people of working age will increase. It is predicted, for example, that by 2020, 60% of people in their 50s will have a disability.

→ Your business will be in a better position to meet the changing needs of customers and clients. Disabled employees can give you a real insight into new markets and can act as the catalyst for development of new products or services.

→ Taking a positive attitude towards the recruitment of disabled people will help to protect your business against claims of discrimination.

→ A disability-confident approach will enhance your reputation as an employer and within your wider community.

So, as you can see, there's a really strong business case for looking at the potential and capabilities of a diverse pool of candidates, rather than focusing on the fact that someone may have a disability or long-term health condition.

Disability facts

- One in every eight UK employees has a disability – that's 3.3 million people.
- Two per cent of the working-age UK population become disabled every year.
- Seventy-eight per cent of people acquire their disability at the age of 16 or older.
- One in every 11 students who graduate each year has a disability.

Disability – what do we mean?

Mention the word "disability" and most people immediately think of someone in a wheelchair. In fact, the term "disability" covers a wide range of conditions and only a very small percentage of people who are classed as disabled are wheelchair users.

It's useful to look at the definition of disability given in the Equality Act 2010:

> [A] person is disabled if they have a physical or mental impairment which has a substantial and long-term adverse affect on their ability to carry out normal day-to-day activities.

Long-term means that the condition must last, or be likely to last, for more than 12 months or that it is terminal.

What this demonstrates is that not all disabilities are obvious. In fact many businesses are already employing people who would be defined as disabled without even realising it. Sometimes this is because the individual has chosen not to use the term "disabled" to describe themselves, or because they simply don't want to tell their employer about an issue for fear they would be treated differently. There is still, for example, an enormous stigma attached to mental health problems such as depression, even though they affect a huge number of people and stress-related illnesses are on the increase.

The Equality Act 2010 states that it is unlawful for employers to discriminate against a disabled person in any area of employment, from recruitment and training to promotion and dismissal.

What this means in practice is that you have to ensure that your recruitment processes are fair and do not – even inadvertently – discriminate against disabled people. This isn't difficult to achieve – it just means making sure, for example, that you don't ask applicants to disclose information that is not actually relevant to the job in hand. It also means holding interviews at an accessible venue and asking people if you need to make any adjustments to enable them to attend. A visually impaired person, for example, might need someone to guide them from reception to the interview room. (We talk more about equality in recruitment in Chapter 5.)

You are also obliged to make reasonable adjustments to enable a disabled person who has the right skills to take up the job (see the next section) and to make sure that any of the policies or practices in your business don't indirectly put a disabled person at a disadvantage.

Making reasonable adjustments

Under the Equality Act 2010, businesses are obliged to make "reasonable adjustments" to enable a disabled person to work (or continue working) for them.

In most cases, this just means making simple, small changes that cost little or nothing. The legislation makes it clear that businesses won't be expected to make adjustments which they can't afford or which are not practical. What this means in reality is that the adjustments that are expected will vary from business to business – depending on the cost involved in any adjustment, the practicalities of making the changes and the financial resources available to the business.

Examples of reasonable adjustments you might make to enable a disabled person to work with you could include:

- changing their hours or offering them flexible or part-time work

- providing specialist equipment to help them do their job; perhaps a particular type of chair or workstation or voice-activated software

- giving them an office on the ground floor so that their work area is easily accessible.

The best way to go about deciding what's appropriate is to discuss it with the disabled person themselves. There's also plenty of external help and support – and in some cases funding – to call on (see the next section).

Bear in mind that the need to make reasonable adjustments also applies when someone who is already working with you becomes disabled, or if there is a change in their condition that has an impact on their work.

Every year, 25,000 people in the UK leave work due to injury and ill health, yet 43.7% of disabled Europeans say they could continue to work if their employers made adjustments. That's a huge waste of the investment businesses have already made in talented individuals, whom they seem prepared to allow to walk out of the door for the sake of a few simple changes.

The kinds of adjustments you might make for an existing employee include those listed above, but could also involve reducing working hours, allowing people time off for hospital or rehabilitation appointments or reallocating some of their duties to another member of staff.

In many cases, it should be perfectly possible for someone who has become disabled to continue working for you. But remember that if you do end an employee's contract for reasons that relate to their disability, you have to be able to justify your actions – and you won't be able to do that if it's clear that a few simple changes would make the difference.

Startups Tip
There's plenty of help and support out there for businesses who are positive about employing disabled people. Make sure you take advantage of it.

Help and support

There are two key schemes available to help employers who are planning to take on disabled people.

Access to Work (AtW)

This is a government-run programme that aims to help disabled people overcome some of the barriers they face in getting and keeping jobs.

An adviser will be able to help you assess your employees' needs, and in some cases can help you apply for a financial grant towards the cost of any adjustments you need to make. In some cases, you will be able to recoup all the costs.

The funding could be used to pay for, or put towards, specialist equipment and adaptations to premises. In some cases it can even be used towards the cost of an employee who cannot use public transport to travel to and from work.

The initial application has to be made by the disabled person themselves. Once it's been received and their eligibility confirmed, you will then be allocated a local adviser to help you.

Work Choice

This government-run programme is designed to help disabled people who have more complex issues. Support is available to help businesses provide work of 16 hours or more per week for eligible disabled people. Advisers will work with you to develop a package of support tailored to the individual's needs. You can find out more about this through the Disability Employment Adviser at your local Jobcentre Plus.

The disability symbol

If you're really serious about becoming a disability-positive business, you can apply for the disability symbol.

This is a Kitemark awarded by Jobcentre Plus to employers who commit to meeting certain criteria around the recruitment and employment of disabled people.

The commitments are:

-> to interview all disabled applicants who meet the minimum criteria for a job vacancy and to consider them on their abilities

-> to ensure that there is a mechanism in place to discuss, at any time – but at least once a year – with disabled employees what they can do to make sure they can develop and use their abilities

-> to make every effort when employees become disabled to make sure that they stay in employment

-> to take action to ensure that all employees develop the appropriate level of disability awareness needed to make your commitments work

-> to review your commitments and what has been achieved yearly, planning ways to improve them and letting employees and Jobcentre Plus know about progress and future plans.

In my experience

Stephen Morton, Security Officer

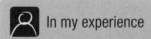

Stephen Morton thought he had turned the corner when Remploy (charity working to increase employment opportunities for disabled people): supported him into work as a security officer with a leading supermarket. But unfortunately for the Wrexham man, he had only been in his new job for a few months when he was made redundant because of the economic downturn. "Through no fault of his own he was back at square one looking for work," said Grace Jackson, manager of Remploy's Wrexham branch. "But Stephen is a determined person and together we set about finding him another job."

"Remploy has always been there for me and I was confident that I wouldn't be out of work for long," said Stephen, who has white finger, an industrial injury caused by continuous use of vibrating hand-held machinery. "One of the first things they did was to arrange for me go on a four-day course for security staff and paid for my SIA licence, which is a key requirement for working in the security sector."

Stephen's employment adviser arranged an interview with local firm Beswick Security, which had a vacancy for a security officer at Wrexham bus station. "The interview went really well and I was offered the job there and then," added Stephen, who also received support from Remploy with interview techniques and CV writing. "I love working in the security sector and I'm really enjoying working at the bus station. Being a local man, I'm also able to help when I get asked about bus times and routes!" He added, "Having experienced unemployment I know how it can dent your confidence and self-esteem. However, I also know that if I was ever in a similar situation in the future Remploy would be there to help."

Useful contacts

- Gov.UK guide to recruiting someone who is disabled: www.gov.uk/recruitment-disabled-people.
- CIPD Factsheet on Disability and Employment: www.cipd.co.uk/hr-resources/factsheets/disability-employment.aspx.
- Employers' Forum on Disability: helpline 020 7403 3020; www.efd.org.uk.
- Remploy www.remploy.co.uk

Checklist

☑ Consider how a disabled employee might help you widen your understanding of customer needs and tap into new markets.

☑ Think about what your business needs to do to become more disability confident.

☑ Review your recruitment advertisements to make sure you are not inadvertently discriminating against disabled candidates.

☑ Gen up on the advice and financial support that is available to employers who take on disabled people.

✐ *CHAPTER 5*

Getting ready to recruit

📖 What's in this chapter?

So you've made a decision to take someone on, and thought about the kind of contractual arrangement to best suit your business, but what are the key actions you need to take before launching into the recruitment process?

In this chapter we'll cover:

→ drawing up a job description that accurately reflects the role
→ putting together a person specification that attracts the right candidates
→ how to make sure you're offering the right rate of pay for the job
→ other benefits you might offer prospective employees
→ deciding on the best place to advertise your vacancy
→ creating a compelling job advert that also complies with the law
→ planning how to manage applications.

Once you've made the big decision to take someone on, it can be tempting to rush headlong into the recruitment process. But there are two more key actions you need to take before you are ready to start advertising the role. You need to draw up a job description and person specification – and you also need to decide how much you are going to pay your new recruit.

Drawing up a job description

There's no legal requirement to draw up a job description, but it's definitely good practice and will help you think more clearly about exactly what it is you want your new recruit to do. You are, however, required to include a job title or job description in the written statement of terms, which you must give to an employee within one month of starting.

Defining the job accurately will also help to ensure that you draw up a realistic job advertisement that will attract candidates with the right skills and qualities.

Sometimes the process of drawing up a job description can help you confirm your thinking about whether you need a full- or part-time person. Once you've listed the tasks and thought about how often they need to be performed, you can make a judgement about the amount of time it will take to fulfil the role.

Of course, once the person is in post, a job description can also help to ensure that there are no misunderstandings about what is required and how the role fits in to the business overall.

A job description should include:

-→ the job title

-→ who the post-holder will report to (or who will report to them)

-→ the main objective of the job

-→ a description of the specific tasks that will be involved on a regular basis

-> an indication of other tasks that may be necessary on an ad hoc/ occasional basis

-> if appropriate, the results that the job-holder will be expected to deliver

-> where the job will be based (ie at your premises, home-based, flexible location).

It's also useful to draw up an accompanying person specification. This is basically a list of the skills, qualities and experience a successful candidate would need to have.

It's important to be realistic about your expectations. Yes, of course you want to find an experienced person who will do a great job and hit the ground running. If you are too exacting in your demands, however, you may be ruling out some really good candidates who could make a valuable contribution to your business.

Think about your own experience of searching and applying for jobs. How often have you seen a role that seemed right up your street, but have been put off from applying because you didn't have a specific qualification or couldn't meet just one of the criteria?

Your person spec should include both skills and personal qualities. A list of skills might include knowledge of a particular computer package, proven telephone sales ability or customer service experience. You may also want to find someone with certain qualities, such as the ability to work independently, to make decisions under pressure or to pay close attention to detail.

When drawing up a job description and person spec, you might find it useful to split your requirements into two parts: those that are "essential" to the role; and those that are "desirable." If you are recruiting an office manager, for example, you might feel that competency in the full Microsoft Office package is essential, but that previous experience of working in your particular industry or sector is only desirable. If you're looking for a salesperson you would most likely want them to have excellent interpersonal skills and a proven track record in closing deals, but although it would be useful if they were bilingual, it wouldn't be a deal-breaker.

It's definitely worth devoting time to thinking carefully about what skills and qualities really are essential. *Recruit for attitude, train for skills* is a mantra worth bearing in mind. Someone may have never worked in your specific sector, but if they have an excellent track record in bringing projects in on time, does it really matter? How long would it really take them to familiarise themselves with the ins and outs of your industry?

Equally, a candidate for a secretarial role may not tick all the boxes in terms of knowledge of specific computer packages, but if they're organised, efficient and capable of keeping all the balls in the air, how hard would it be to send them on a quick training course to get them up to speed?

You can also use this person spec to measure candidates against at the interview stage (we talk more about this in Chapter 6).

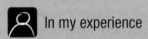 In my experience

Patrick van der Vorst, ValueMyStuff.com

ValueMyStuff.com started as an online service that guaranteed to provide customers with a valuation of their art, paintings, silver, furniture or other antiques and collectables within 48 hours.

It has grown rapidly over the past two years and now also conducts home visits and sells items on clients' behalf. Its American market has expanded significantly and now represents a third of the client base.

The business, which was launched by ex-Sotheby's expert Patrick van der Vorst, successfully secured investment from Theo Paphitis and Deborah Meaden on the TV programme *Dragons' Den* and now employs three people.

Patrick's view is that a clear job description and person specification is vital, but that they need to be draw up with a certain amount of flexibility. "I do put together a clear job description when I am going to employ someone because I think it's both necessary and a fair thing to do. If you have a set list of skills and requirements it means someone comes into the job with a clear goal," he explains.

His experience, however, was that as the business evolved, needs changed and the emphasis of people's jobs shifted. "With a start-up, once some of the initial things are done it frees up time and allows you to move on to the next thing," he says. "The requirements of the job evolve and more tasks get added to the list, so you have to be flexible and responsive as things come along.

"Our business is becoming more complex as we provide more different services to a larger group of clients. So I think what will happen is that we will move from general roles to more specialised job specifications where people focus on a key area of expertise."

Patrick adds that good communication is the key to making sure existing staff are on board with any changes. "We sit down every month and have an update, go through the job requirements and anything new that is needed in the role," he says. "As a small business we keep everything out in the open. If there are any concerns or worries we sit down and talk about them immediately so there are no surprises."

Deciding how much to pay

Even in times of recession, recruitment is a competitive business. Candidates are vying for the best jobs and employers are competing for the best people for those positions.

Taking on a new employee is a major step for a start-up and you'll want the best person, whatever the role is.

To achieve this you will have to pay the going rate, or close to it; but what is the going rate, and is pay the only factor that will swing the deal?

Before looking into these points, it is worth evaluating the job you plan to offer in terms of the responsibilities of the role and the know-how you want the candidate to possess. This will help you gauge what to pay.

Evaluating the job

Is it a specialist job or a basic admin role? Will the new recruit be juggling a range of activities and resources, requiring planning and organisational skills? Will the problems they face day to day be simple and repetitive or complex and ever-changing? How much responsibility will they have to make decisions?

Big companies use evaluation schemes like the Hay method to "score" jobs so that comparable jobs can be grouped in pay bands across the organisation. It's not necessary to take such a formal approach for your first recruit, but thinking about these points will help you assess the value of the job and the pay that would be commensurate with that role.

Pay variations

Other factors that come into the equation include location, professional qualifications and experience.

It's a postcode lottery when it comes to pay. If your business is based in London you will pay more, but if your start-up is in Northern Ireland, for example, an average weekly wage could be £200 a week less than the national average. (At the time of writing, the Office for National Statistics (ONS) puts the national average at £467.)

If you are looking for skilled professionals you will have to pay more. According to the ONS, the highest earners in 2010 were health professionals, followed by corporate managers and science and technology professionals. The lowest paid were those in sales occupations.

Experience is perhaps a little more difficult to quantify, which is why employers often set a salary range for the job so that they can take this and other factors into account when they get to the point of making a job offer.

> ### Startups Tip
> For information about average earnings in your region, check out the Annual Survey of Hours and Earnings published by ONS (www.ons. gov.uk).

Basic pay

The National Minimum Wage is another useful benchmark to help you set basic pay. This is set at different levels depending on age. At the time of writing the levels were:

-> £6.19 per hour for workers aged 21 and over

-> £4.98 per hour for 18 to 20-year-olds

-> £3.68 for 16–17-year-old workers above school leaving age but under 18

-> £2.65 for apprentices under 19 or 19 or over and in the first year of their apprenticeship.

These rates are reviewed annually by the Low Pay Commission, so you need to keep an eye out for any changes.

While these are minimum rates that almost all workers are entitled to be paid, there is nothing stopping you paying above the minimum wage.

For the latest information visit www.gov.uk/your-right-to-minimum-wage.

Higher earners

Skilled workers, professionals and those with relevant experience command higher rewards. Many professional bodies publish regular pay surveys providing a benchmark on which to base salary scales.

The main findings are usually freely available on the internet. For example, the Institute of Chartered Accountants in England and Wales publishes an annual Career Benchmarking Survey with employment consultancy Robert Half (see www.icaew.com).

Information about managers' pay is provided by the National Management Salary Survey, published annually by the Chartered Management Institute (CMI) and XpertHR. The 2011 report shows that the average "executive" salary was £36,413, but for more detailed information you will have to buy a copy of the report: email salarysurveys@xperthr.co.uk.

Other sources

Job sites are another good source of information on salaries. If you decide to place your ad with a recruitment agency, they will be able to provide you with advice about the going rate for the job you wish to advertise.

Affordability

As with any expense in life, you are likely to be constrained by what your budding business can actually afford. You also want the maximum bang for your buck. To determine what you can afford, you need to consider carefully the value to your business of the gap this person will fill and what impact they will have on the bottom line.

Taking on a general admin person may be less expensive than employing someone with the skills to help your business grow, but it could be a false economy in the long run.

Employment package

The salary you are able to offer is very important, but it is not the only criterion on which individuals base job choice decisions. Career opportunities, the challenge of the role, job security, flexible working and other "benefits in kind" all influence the candidate's decision. So it's important to consider the other incentives you may have to offer in your remuneration package, not just pay, to appeal to the type of candidate you really want to attract.

Health insurance, dental insurance, company car, childcare vouchers, tuition reimbursement, time off to study, season ticket loans, additional holiday purchase scheme, share scheme, one Friday afternoon off a month … these and other ideas could be included in a range of benefit options you make available to your new employee. Make sure, though, that any benefits you do offer reflect the values of your business and are compatible with your operation.

Remember also that there are tax and NIC implications for any benefits in kind you provide to employees. Working out the total cost of your remuneration package is vital before you start advertising the role.

Incentives

We've all read about mind-bogglingly large bankers' bonuses, but more modest schemes are run by many businesses to incentivise and reward performance.

If you do decide to introduce bonuses, commission on sales or performance-related pay rewards, make sure the scheme is fair, equitable, set against measurable targets and clearly communicated. And don't move the goalposts halfway through the year unless you want to make your staff very unhappy.

For more information about performance-related pay schemes, visit www.cipd.co.uk/hr-resources/factsheets/performance-related-pay.aspx.

Stakeholding

Giving employees a stake in the business is probably the ultimate incentive. The John Lewis Partnership is a shining example of this principle in practice. John Lewis says that being a partnership business is about much more than sharing the profits.

It defines our approach to what we do. With ownership comes responsibility, and the knowledge that our success depends entirely on providing the best quality products and services to our customers so that they come back to us again and again.

You may not yet be quite as big as John Lewis, but giving employees a stake in the business is an option for a smaller business.

For more information about employee ownership, visit www.employeeownership.co.uk.

The whole package

As mentioned earlier, pay isn't the only incentive a small, growing business has to offer. The opportunity to be in at the start of something new has great appeal for many people. In a recent survey, 83% of managers cited the challenge of the job as the main reason for taking on their current role.

The type of business you are or the products you sell could also provide a unique selling point (USP). Social enterprises, charities, eco-businesses and internet-based start-ups tick all the boxes for many job-seekers. Whatever your USP, make sure you identify it and clearly promote it in your job advertisement.

Equal pay

The latest equality legislation may seem like a potential minefield for the small employer, but it is based on a simple principle – fairness. If you approach it from this standpoint, it should be relatively simple to negotiate your way through all the legal obligations covered by the Equality Act 2010 in your dealings with employees.

The Act covers equal pay, which is defined by the Equality and Human Rights Commission (EHRC) as:

. . . ensuring that what you pay your employees is not affected, even unintentionally, by factors such as their sex, their race, or whether they have a disability.

Outdated work practices, expectations and stereotypes, differences in working patterns because of the caring role of many women, and a lack of quality part-time work are all cited as reasons why gender pay discrimination exists.

The Commission has developed an online "equal pay toolkit" for small businesses to use: you can find this via www.equalityhumanrights.com.

The Advisory, Conciliation and Arbitration Service (Acas) also publishes an advisory booklet on pay systems which provides useful advice: www.Acas.org.uk/index.aspx?articleid=716.

> Forty years after the original Equal Pay Act, women working full-time in the UK are still paid on average 14.9% less per hour than men, according to the Fawcett Society (www.fawcettsociety.org.uk).

Planning ahead

No one wants to be stuck on the same salary for ever, so you do need to give some thought as to when you are going to review an employee's salary and how you will make decisions about what level of increase to give. To do this you will need to review pay and benefits with your employee at least once a year. Make sure that you:

⇢ recognise and reward achievement

⇢ ensure that pay reviews are transparent and fair

⇢ make appraisal meetings two-way conversations

⇢ put a scalable system in place.

In the future you may be in a position to take on more staff, and if you have put careful thought into the pay and benefits of your first employee (based firmly on their skills and experience and the going rate for the job), any future employees should slot into the structured pay band that you have carefully established for the business.

- Make sure you have a clear job description for the role, which covers all the key tasks and responsibilities.
- Think carefully about the person specification and decide which skills and qualities are "essential" as opposed to "desirable".
- Gen up on local and professional pay rates to help you set a fair salary for the job.
- Make sure you are up to date on and complying with legislation on the National Minimum Wage and equal pay.
- Think about what other incentives and/or benefits you could offer to make the job appealing to candidates.
- Plan ahead for how you will "scale" the salary when the time comes to review your employee's pay.

Working hours

In drawing up your job description, you will no doubt have come to a decision about the number of hours you would like your prospective new recruit to work. This is something you might want to negotiate with a candidate, but it makes sense to have an idea of what your ideal scenario is and how far you are willing to depart from it.

It is very important to be absolutely clear about what the working hours are, whether or not overtime will be paid if your employee works over those hours, and the rate at which overtime will be paid.

There are statutory rights regarding maximum working hours as well as holiday entitlement. Workers aged 18 and over are entitled to:

→ 5.6 weeks' holiday a year

→ work no more than six days out of every seven, or 12 out of every 14

→ take a 20-minute break if their shift lasts for more than six hours

→ work a maximum 48-hour average week.

Workers aged 16 to 17 are entitled to:

→ take at least 30 minutes' break if their shift lasts more than four and a half hours

--> work no more than eight hours a day and 40 hours a week

--> have 12 hours' rest between working days and two days off every week

--> 5.6 weeks' holiday a year.

If the job you are offering is part-time, these entitlements need to be calculated on a pro rata basis, eg 16.8 days' holiday per year for someone working three days a week.

These entitlements, which are governed by the EU Working Time Regulations, cover part-time, casual, freelance and agency staff. Certain sectors are subject to different rules and in some situations workers may opt out of the working time limits. Visit the Acas website for further information about exemptions and opt-outs to the directive (www.acas.org.uk/index.aspx?articleid=1373).

> Be clear about exactly how many hours you want your new employee to work – and how this fits with the regulations around working time.

Advertising your vacancy

Gone are the days when the only way to advertise a job vacancy was an expensive advert in the local newspaper or trade press. That's not to say that the printed media is no longer an effective route. In many cases it can still yield excellent results – but there is now a whole raft of other options available to help you find the right candidate.

The key is to think creatively about which recruitment medium or method will work best for your business and your budget and is most likely to attract the kind of candidate you are looking for.

When you are weighing up the options, you need to think carefully about the following issues.

--> How quickly do you need a response?

--> How long do you want the job advert to run for?

-> How much are you prepared to pay to advertise?

-> Is one type of advertising likely to be sufficient, or would it be better to use a combination of outlets?

-> Is the job vacancy most likely to attract a local candidate, or do you want to spread the word to people further afield?

-> What specialist media is your ideal candidate likely to read?

-> What online communities are they likely to be involved in?

Thinking this through will help you decide which of the following options, or combination of options, will best meet your needs.

Local advertising

You will undoubtedly already be aware of your local free or paid-for newspaper and in the past may even have scanned the jobs pages yourself.

Larger towns often have more than one local paper, so make sure you familiarise yourself with what's available and look carefully at the circulation figures and the areas covered. Check whether the newspaper has a supporting website that could also carry your advert – many of them do. Many local papers are part of a wider publishing group, so you may also be able to arrange for your advert to be carried in sister newspapers in neighbouring towns.

Scanning the papers will also give you an idea of the kind of jobs that are typically advertised for locally and the average salary range for your area.

Print advertising can be quite expensive, but because local papers are widely read, you are likely to get a good response, particularly if you are advertising for a general role such as an administrator or salesperson. You need to bear in mind, however, that this is not a particularly targeted form of advertising. The newspaper will go to everyone in the area, and unless your advert is very specific, you may have to wade through a lot of unsuitable applicants or deal with an avalanche of phone calls.

Prices vary from region to region, but the procedure is largely the same. You fax or email the text of your advert through and an advertising rep will call you back to discuss the options and give you a price.

Make sure you always see a proof copy of your advert, particularly if you have phoned it through. It's very easy to mishear over the phone, and an advert that's littered with mistakes or spelling errors won't give a good impression of your business.

Recruitment howlers

Wanted: Three year old teacher needed for private nursery. Experience preferred.

Wanted: Administrator. Peasant working conditions.

If you're looking to place a very simple small advert, you will probably be charged by the line, for example £17 per line plus VAT. Each line will probably have no more than four or five words in it, so there isn't scope to say a great deal, but you could get a simple message across. The average cost of a small boxed advert in a local paper would be around £300, and obviously the larger the box the higher the price.

Think carefully about the timing before you place your advert. You are unlikely to get the best return for your investment if you advertise around a public holiday, for example, when lots of people will be away and the paper is probably producing a condensed edition.

The local newspaper isn't your only option for reaching a local audience. Depending on the nature of your vacancy, you could also consider local community magazines, newsagents' windows and supermarket noticeboards. Of course, if you have premises yourself, such as a shop or an office with a street front, you could always put a notice up in your own door or window. Bear in mind, however, that people will not necessarily see this kind of advert immediately, so it won't work if you are looking for someone in a hurry.

Trade and professional press

There are magazines and newspapers covering just about every profession, from engineering and catering to personnel and finance. You will almost certainly be aware of the magazines that cover your own specialist sector and will be able to make a judgement about whether it's worth investing in an advert.

If you are recruiting for a profession outside your area of expertise – say you need a marketing person or an IT whizz, for example – you will be able to find a full listing of relevant press in *Willings Press Guide*, which you will find in most good local libraries.

Some national newspapers also have supplements on particular days of the week. The *Guardian*, for example, runs media job adverts on a Monday, while the *Sunday Times* has an appointments section advertising senior roles.

Once again, this type of print advertising is not cheap. An advert for an HR person in *People Management*, for example, would cost £5,100 for a quarter page mono (black and white) advert. It is, however, a targeted type of advertising and could well net you exactly the type of applicants you are looking for. Like their local newspaper counterparts, many sector magazines and newspaper supplements also have supporting websites which can help to extend the reach of your advert.

If you are not familiar with the magazines you are considering, request a couple of back issues so that you can compare competing publications and see what kind of jobs are advertised. Ask detailed questions about circulation, publication frequency and the breakdown of readership (eg levels of seniority), and don't be afraid to negotiate on price. It's a competitive market and you will undoubtedly be able to improve on the first price you are quoted.

Jobcentre Plus

Don't overlook your local Jobcentre when it comes to seeking candidates. There are over a thousand Jobcentres across the country that can help you find people for a whole range of positions. You can post your vacancy for free using the Employer Direct service. Details of the job will be displayed:

- ⇢ on the jobsearch facility on the gov.uk website
- ⇢ through Jobseeker Direct – a phone service for people applying for jobs
- ⇢ on the network of electronic touch-screen terminals that can be found in Jobcentre Plus offices and in local communities across Britain. It is estimated that these are used by more than 1.5 million people looking for work each week.

To use the Employer Direct service, telephone 0845 601 2001 with details of your vacancy. A textphone service is available for people with speech or hearing impediments (0845 601 2002). You can also email details of your vacancy via employerdirect-vacancies@jobcentreplus.gsi.gov.uk.

Jobcentre Plus also runs Employer Direct online, a free internet service that enables you to post vacancies online 24/7 without having to speak to an adviser. To use this service visit www.gov.uk/employer-direct-online. You can use the service as an *approved user* or an *unapproved user*.

Registering as an approved user can save time and will help you manage the process of advertising jobs more efficiently. It means that online job notification forms will be pre-populated with your company details and you can view, copy and amend jobs that you have notified with Jobcentre Plus over the previous year.

If you are an unapproved user, you will need to complete the job notification form in full every time you register a vacancy. If you want to make any amendments to an advert, you have to do this by calling the contact centre staff.

If you have a vacancy in a field where there is a skills shortage, Jobcentre Plus can also help you recruit from other countries in Europe through its European Employment Services (EURES). To take advantage of these services, you need to ensure that you are offering at least national minimum wage rates and that your vacancy is fully compliant with UK employment and equality legislation.

Jobcentre Plus can also offer a wealth of advice and information to help you with the recruitment process. Recruitment advisers can:

--> provide advice on issues such as the local job market, training, equal opportunities and specialist types of employment

--> give you access to Jobcentre Plus offices to conduct your interviews

--> provide specialist support on recruiting and retaining the skills of disabled workers

--> help you sort through application forms and select candidates for interview

--> help you try out employees without risk by offering work trials to potential candidates.

Recruitment agencies

Another option is to place your vacancy with a local or specialist recruitment agency. Agencies hold databases of job-seekers and may already have people on their books who fit the bill. They can also advertise the vacancy for you and help sift and shortlist applicants, saving you valuable time. Recruitment consultancies will also conduct basic checks on candidates to confirm their identity and eligibility to work.

This is an expensive route, but a good agency can introduce you to strong candidates you might not otherwise have found. They can also guide you through the recruitment process if it's an area where you are feeling a little out of your depth.

If you decide to work with an agency, make sure you choose your supplier with care. As with any industry, you will find many excellent practitioners (and a few unscrupulous ones who could seriously damage your company's reputation). The following questions will help you make an informed decision about which agency to work with.

--> Are they a member of the Recruitment and Employment Confederation (REC) (the industry's professional body)? REC member agencies work to a code of professional practice and have regular independent inspections to make sure their performance is up to scratch. You can find local, regional and specialist member agencies listed on the REC's website, www.rec.uk.com.

-> Are the consultants employed by the agency professionally qualified? There are two government-approved recruitment industry qualifications: the Certificate in Recruitment Practice, and the Diploma in Recruitment Practice. If the consultant you are working with holds either of these qualifications, it would suggest that they are well versed in recruitment law and up to date with best practice.

-> Does the agency have a clear complaints procedure? In the unlikely event of any problems during your relationship with them there should be an established process to follow.

-> Does your vacancy call for a recruitment agency with general, local knowledge or would you be better working with consultants who have specific sector or industry expertise? You will find specialist agencies dealing in a range of sectors, from accountancy and engineering to sales and human resources. The REC website will help you source an appropriate provider.

-> Do you need local, regional or national coverage for your vacancy? If you are advertising a low-key admin role, for example, a small local agency could be a good bet. If you are recruiting for a specialist role or a position that has a flexible location, you might want to consider a recruitment consultancy that has a network of regional offices and can give you national reach.

-> Does the recruitment agency you are considering have a good reputation? It's worth looking beyond the glossy brochure and flash website and seeking some informal feedback from people who have used their services in the past. Don't be afraid to ask the agency if you can speak to some of its past clients directly. You need to be confident that the agency will represent your business well during the recruitment process.

-> What added-value services does the agency provide? Recruitment agencies nowadays provide a range of services, from the basic introduction and short-listing of candidates to sophisticated psychometric testing and advice on employment law. Make sure you know exactly what's available and what you are getting for your money.

-> Does the recruitment agency have an open, honest approach? Make sure they are transparent about terms and fees, realistic about timescales and will communicate with you regularly about progress.

It's important to recognise that any relationship with a supplier is a two-way partnership. You need to be clear about what you are looking for, realistic about what can be achieved and willing to listen to your recruitment consultant's expert advice.

Fee structures vary from agency to agency, but any reputable supplier should provide you with their terms and conditions of business up front.

The most common types of fee arrangement are listed below.

Permanent placement fees

If you are looking to recruit a permanent candidate you would generally expect to pay a fixed fee for the agency's help. Normally, this fee is payable in thirds:

-> one-third up front when the work is commissioned

-> one-third on production of a viable shortlist

-> one-third on successful offer, acceptance and (if applicable) resignation of the candidate from the previous post.

> ### Startups Tip
> Check the recruitment agency's terms carefully. Will they offer a refund of the placement fee if a candidate they have introduced leaves soon after being hired?

Bear in mind that you will probably also have to pay any other costs associated with the recruitment process. If you asked an agency to run a series of adverts in the relevant professional press, for example, you would be expected to foot the bill for that campaign.

Make sure you are really clear from the outset about exactly what is and isn't included in the fee.

Temp to perm fees

You may decide to try out someone introduced by the agency on a temporary basis, with a view to taking them on permanently if it works out well. In this scenario, you would typically be charged what is known as a "temp to perm" fee. The amount of this fee varies from agency to agency, so if you are entering into this kind of arrangement make sure you are clear about costs from the start.

It's worth knowing that if you would prefer not to pay that flat fee, the agency is required by law to give you the alternative of an "extended period of hire". Basically this means that the employee continues to be employed on a temporary contract by the agency for a further fixed period of time, after which they can transfer to your permanent employ.

The recruitment industry has gone through a great deal of change in recent years in response to the challenging marketplace and the increase in web-based recruiting. New ways of working are emerging, and you may find agencies using different fee structures from the ones outlined above, particularly if they specialise in more senior level recruitment. Some, for example, charge a minimum percentage fee up front and the balance after the successful candidate has been in post for a substantial period, say six months.

The key for you is to make sure you have a full understanding of what you are paying for and how it will be charged before you engage in a relationship with a recruitment agency.

Internet job boards

The internet is becoming an increasingly popular tool for recruitment. Research suggests that at least one-third of people who are job-hunting look at web-based job boards to find suitable vacancies.

These online job boards vary in the way they work and the range of services they offer to candidates and clients. Generally, however, they charge companies to place job adverts and allow job-seekers to access information about vacancies for free.

If you think this kind of advertising might work for you, it's worth visiting some of the key sites to get a feel for how they work.

 Startups Tip

Have a look at some of the online job boards:

www.jobsearch.co.uk
www.jobsite.co.uk
www.monster.co.uk
www.reed.co.uk
www.stepstone.com

There are hundreds more job sites covering specific industry areas. A quick internet search will turn up the key websites for your particular field.

Most sites go beyond just offering employers the facility to post vacancies. You will typically also be able to buy access to a database of CVs and conduct tailored searches of possible candidates based on criteria such as location, skills, job titles, etc. Some sites offer a "matching" service (ie they do the search on your behalf and send you suitable CVs) or can even email potential candidates on your behalf with details of your vacancy. Many job boards offer advice and resources to help you with the recruitment process – some even allow you to post videos about your company to give candidates a taste of what it might be like to work for you.

Posting vacancies is generally quite straightforward. In most cases you simply register on the site, email the details of your vacancy and pay online by debit or credit card.

Of course, all these services come at a price, but basic online advertising is generally cheaper than print, particularly if you want to reach a national audience.

Some online job sites do have services which are targeted specifically at small businesses. At the time of writing, for example, Monster was advertising a specific product allowing small businesses to advertise certain types of vacancy for £99 for a period of 14 days.

Bear in mind that people tend to be less discriminating when they are applying for jobs via online recruitment sites. It only takes a few minutes to send off your CV, and job-hunters will often take pot luck and apply for anything that's going. That means you may have to weed through lots of unsuitable applications to find a few gems.

Social media sites

You may love them or hate them, but you certainly can't ignore the presence and influence of social media sites such as Facebook, LinkedIn and Twitter.

Many larger businesses regularly use these sites to attract candidates for specific vacancies and to build up an ongoing dialogue with talented people who may one day want to work for them.

Social networking sites, however, are not just a tool for the big corporates. Used sensibly, they can also be a valuable recruitment tool for small businesses.

LinkedIn

LinkedIn (www.linkedin.com) is an online professional network. It has over five million members in the UK, most of them at managerial or professional level. It's free to join, but you can opt to upgrade to a paid subscription, which provides increased access to potentially useful contacts.

Members use LinkedIn to make useful connections, keep in touch with their network, raise their profile, and promote their expertise, products or services. LinkedIn also provides a valuable opportunity through its specialist groups for its members to discuss topical issues and keep up to date with developments in their specific industry.

You may already have a personal presence on LinkedIn (and if not, it's definitely worth considering) and depending on the nature of your business, you may even have set up a special interest group to help you communicate with clients, contacts and fellow professionals.

If you are already on LinkedIn, spreading the word about your vacancy is easy. You can simply let your existing network of contacts know that you are looking to hire by posting an update or making details of the vacancy available on any groups you host or belong to. This is a great way of attracting passive candidates – those who are not actively job-hunting but who may like the sound of the role you have highlighted.

If you don't have an established presence or your network is very small, you might want to consider paying to post a vacancy. It's a very simple process. Just click on the "Jobs" tab at the top of the LinkedIn home page. If you choose to "post a job" it will take you through to a template where you can enter details of your vacancy and the type of person you are looking for. It costs £195 for a 30-day listing, which will make your job vacancy accessible to LinkedIn members who are searching for jobs in a specific field.

LinkedIn does offer a range of more sophisticated recruitment tools, but these are likely to be of more interest further down the line, when your business has grown and you are recruiting regularly or for multiple vacancies.

Facebook

Don't overlook the potential of Facebook for recruiting. Facebook has over 25 million users in the UK – that's almost half the population. It is the second most visited website in the UK, behind Google, and the age profile may surprise you: 60% of users are 26 or older and nearly 20% are 45 or older.

Large corporates have already switched on to the power of Facebook, with many setting up specific career and recruitment groups on the site. It's becoming an increasingly popular way of recruiting graduates, for example, who are comfortable with social networking and like to access and share information online.

As a small business taking on your first one or two employees, you're unlikely to want to launch a large-scale, paid-for recruitment campaign on Facebook. But remember that by its very nature, Facebook is viral and can help you very quickly spread the message about the job you have on offer. And it's not just your personal contacts who can help you – customers or clients can be potential employees too.

Obviously you need to already be active on Facebook to take full advantage of this. Perhaps you already have a large personal network, or have set up a Facebook group for your business. If so, it's a case of simply letting all your contacts know that you're on the look-out for new staff and directing them to your website (or to you personally) for further information. Even if your contacts aren't interested themselves, they will undoubtedly share the information with their own networks or with friends and family.

Twitter

There's still a great deal of cynicism about Twitter, which, for the uninitiated, is a social networking and micro-blogging service that allows you to answer the question "What are you doing?" by sending short text messages – no more than 140 characters – to your friends or "followers". These messages (called tweets) are a way of quickly sharing information with like-minded people who are in your circle of contacts.

If you're already on Twitter and have a network of followers, it makes sense to use it to spread the word about your vacancy. A quick tweet mentioning that you are offering a job opportunity could quickly spread among your contacts – and, once again it's not just who you know, it's who they know.

If you haven't yet dipped your toe in the water of Twitter, you'll find plenty of advice and information on how to use it for business on the website, www.twitter.com.

The personal touch

It's quite common for small businesses not to bother advertising their vacancy at all. Hiring can often be a bit of a "distress" decision, and the need for speed, coupled with the fact that people often feel uncertain about the hiring process, means that in the early days they often recruit family members or friends.

A word of caution here. This will certainly save money in recruitment costs and it certainly makes sense to look at your immediate circle to see if there is anyone suitable and available. Sometimes it works out fantastically well – but it can also go horribly wrong. Family working relationships can cause tensions, and friends don't always have the same persona at work as they do in the pub. It can be incredibly difficult if you take a friend on and subsequently have to sack them because they are not performing in the role.

> ### Startups Tip
> If you are considering hiring someone you know, make absolutely sure they are the best person for the job.

 In my experience

Sean Scott, Vuba Group

Yorkshire-based Vuba Group supplies and installs industrial flooring and maintenance products. It was set up two years ago by Sean Scott, who made a conscious decision to employ only people he knew personally or who came highly recommended by friends.

"I just felt it wasn't worth taking the risk with someone I didn't know," he explains. "We just didn't have the time or budget to hire someone, get them set up and working, only to find it didn't work out and to have to start all over again."

The business has a team of five, with two office-based staff and a crew of three working out on site. The fact that all the employees were known to Sean led to a very informal approach, which he quickly realised would have to change.

"The majority of people we employ are older than me, and because it had become very informal I sometimes felt I wasn't being listened to," he says. "Our office manager also felt at one point that she was being treated as a bit of a lackey, and when we sat down and talked about it we realised that it just came from the fact that we were all a bit too informal.

"My strongest advice if you are employing people you know would be to take a formal approach right from the start and don't expect things of people because you are their friend. We try and take a much more professional attitude now and everything has worked out fine."

 In my experience

Paul Davies, Positive Solutions

Paul Davies is an independent financial adviser who recently set up a limited liability partnership (LLP) with a colleague under the Positive Solutions umbrella. The business employs Paul's wife Karen to run the office – an arrangement which works well and makes business sense, but is not without its issues.

"The advantage is that I can have utmost trust in Karen. If I have anything sensitive that has to be done, I don't have to be careful about minding my p's and q's so in that respect it's absolutely fantastic.

"The disadvantage is that being husband and wife and employer and employee is not necessarily the best mix. It does have its tensions and if you're not careful it can take its toll on the relationship. We have actually got quite good now at switching off the conversation and being husband and wife outside the office and employer and employee inside the office."

Paul adds that he would be very careful about employing other family members in the future. "These are volatile times we are living in, and if I ever had to make a family member or friend redundant I couldn't look them in the eye afterwards," he says.

Creating a job advert

Once you've decided how to get the message out about your job, the next step is to create a job advertisement.

The nature and exact form of the advert will depend on where you are placing the advert, but there are some basic principles to follow.

A good job advertisement needs to be as follows.

-> **Concise but informative.** Keep it brief, but make sure you include enough information to help candidates decide whether they should apply (ie where the job is based, what skills and experience are required). Use your job description and person specification (see p. 48) to guide you on the key points you need to include.

-> **Attractively designed.** Think carefully about the typeface, type size and general layout. Make sure you use your logo if you have one. The aim should be to produce an advertisement that is easy to read and attractive to look at. If you're advertising in a newspaper or magazine, they will usually be able to give you guidance on this and in many cases can handle the design for you if you wish.

-> **Legal and non-discriminatory.** By law, employers must not discriminate on the grounds of age, race, sex, marriage, disability, gender, sexual orientation or religion or belief. This applies to all businesses and all stages of the recruitment process, including the job advert. We talk more about this on p. 76.

-> **Compelling.** Remember that the idea of the advert is to attract as many good-quality applicants as possible. So focus on the benefits and make it as compelling as you can. Highlight the financial package, any benefits you are planning to offer and the training and development you will provide. (See p. 75 for more on the debate about whether to mention the actual salary or not.) Ask yourself, "If I were looking for a job in this field, would I be tempted to apply?" Some examples of how you can turn a boring advert into a compelling one are given below.

Examples of adverts

Compare excerpts from these two job adverts and see which one would be more likely to spark your interest.

Beauty therapist needed for small local salon. Must be able to cover full range of treatments.

Or:

Enthusiastic beauty therapist needed to join our rapidly growing salon. We are looking for someone with the skills and experience to deliver a full range of leading-edge treatments to our established client base. Ongoing opportunities to train and develop new skills and take on management responsibilities.

- **Written in an appropriate tone.** Make sure the tone of the advert reflects the personality of your business. Should it be serious and formal or jovial and light-hearted? Look at other recruitment advertisements to give you some idea about how to word the advert and position your business. Setting the right tone will help you attract the kind of applicants who are likely to fit in well with your business.

- **Clear about what people need to do next.** Make sure the advert explains how you want people to respond. Do they need to send for an application form or provide a CV? Are you willing to take phone calls or would you prefer them to visit your website for more information? Don't forget to include a deadline for receiving applications. (You'll find more about the application process starting on p. 78.)

The salary – to mention or not to mention?

People are often unsure about whether to mention money in a job advertisement. Scan the recruitment pages in your local press and you'll see that some adverts state a figure, some mention a salary range and others don't say anything at all!

From an applicant's point of view, a complete lack of reference to money can be off-putting. They don't want to waste time putting together a detailed application only to find that the salary is way below the level they are looking for, but equally, they don't want to ring up and ask how much for fear of being seen as a bit money-grabbing and only interested in the financial reward.

From your point of view, if you don't give some indication of pay you are likely to have to wade through lots of applications from people whose salary expectations are way beyond what you're prepared to pay – or who are inappropriate for the level of job you are offering.

If you don't want to mention an actual figure, it's worth at least mentioning a salary range. This gives applicants some idea of what level of reward the job is offering – and gives you the opportunity to fix the final salary at a level appropriate to the successful candidate. Of course, it also means you have put some parameters in place if you decide you want to negotiate in order to secure a particularly talented and experienced employee.

Keeping your job advert legal

Your job advert needs to comply with the terms laid down in the Equality Act, an important piece of legislation which came into force in October 2010.

The Act states that all stages of the recruitment process must treat all races and sexes equally.

The EHRC puts it succinctly.

> If you are recruiting someone to work for you, equality law applies to you:
> –▷ whatever the size of your organisation
> –▷ whatever sector you work in
> –▷ whether you are taking on your first worker, or your hundred and first
> –▷ whether or not you use any formal procedures like application forms, shortlisting or interviewing.

In practical terms, this means that when you advertise, you must not give the impression that you *intend* to discriminate. So instead of advertising for a "waitress", you should advertise for "waiting staff" or "waiter or waitress" to avoid direct discrimination based on sex.

The same principles apply when it comes to age. You cannot stipulate upper or lower age limits for applicants, and you also need to be careful about using terms like "youthful", "dynamic" or "mature", which suggest that you might exclude someone from applying for your job because of their age.

Disability discrimination is an issue too. Make sure the language and/ or criteria you are using don't unwittingly exclude a disabled candidate from applying. There will be some roles for which physical activity, for example, is crucial, but make sure it is a genuine necessity rather than something that is just desirable.

Racial discrimination is another area you need to be aware of. Language skills, for example, may be a crucial part of your role, but you should advertise for someone who is fluent in the language rather than someone who is from a particular country. So you would ask for someone who is "Italian-speaking" rather than "Italian", for example.

There are some exceptions to these rules.

- → **Occupational requirements.** If there is a genuine need for a person of a particular gender or religious background, for example, to perform a role, you can state that only people who meet those characteristics can apply. An example of this might be a women's refuge which is hiring support workers and only wants to employ women in this role. The refuge would probably be able to demonstrate quite clearly that it would only be appropriate for women to apply and that it was a genuine occupational requirement.

- → **The requirement to obey another law.** A driving school looking to hire a driving instructor is one of the examples most commonly used to illustrate this exception. Under the law, driving instructors must be aged at least 21, so it would be acceptable to cite a minimum age.

It is a complex area – but there is plenty of information and guidance available to help you get to grips with the law. You'll find lots of help and information on the EHRC website (www. equalityhumanrights.com).

The organisation that publishes your advert – whether it's a newspaper, magazine or website – is also responsible for making sure the material it carries on your behalf meets legal requirements. Most will have a checking and approval process in place, but don't rely on this – you need to be clear about your responsibilities too.

The application process

Equality legislation also applies to the application process, so if you are considering putting together a formal application form, make sure you are not asking questions that could make you vulnerable to claims of discrimination.

A good rule of thumb is not to ask for personal information that would be inappropriate to use when you are making a decision. So don't ask people to state their date of birth, for example, or to reveal their marital status.

You don't need that information to help you decide if someone is suitable for the job. You will need those personal details if you decide to hire someone, but you can ask for them at a later stage, when the candidate is formally appointed.

It's worth giving some thought to how to manage the application process, and in particular whether to invite CVs or ask people to complete a standard form. There are pros and cons to both approaches.

Application forms:

-→   ensure you get all the basic information you need to make a decision about who to shortlist and interview

-> make it easy for you to compare the skills and experience of candidates who apply for the job

-> can be used again for any future vacancies.

But...

-> you will have to take the time to get one designed and printed

-> you may have to pay to send it out to applicants (although you can produce a .pdf version which can be downloaded from your website)

-> some candidates may be put off by the need to spend time filling in a form.

CVs:

-> demonstrate a candidate's ability to present themselves well (or otherwise) in writing

-> provide a snapshot of an applicant's skills and experience

-> allow you to collect applications more speedily.

But...

-> it is harder to compare the skills and experience of different applicants because the information won't be presented in a consistent format

-> you may have to wade through a lot of irrelevant detail

-> you may get a greater number of unsuitable applications – people tend to fire off CVs on the off-chance, even if they know the job is unlikely to be for them. They will think more carefully about applying if they have to take the time to fill in an application form.

Whichever route you decide to take, you should make sure it is clear to applicants exactly what they need to do to apply and when the deadline is.

Think carefully about whether you will take telephone enquiries. An informal chat can help applicants screen themselves out if they are not what you are looking for. Equally, it can attract a promising candidate further and encourage them to take the trouble to apply.

On the other hand, if your vacancy is likely to attract a large number of applicants, you could spend hours fielding phone calls. If you are expecting a large response, think carefully about how you will manage applications and be realistic about how much time this is likely to take.

It is good practice to at least acknowledge receipt of all applications for your job. Otherwise candidates are left hanging in mid-air – wondering if you have received it, but reluctant to call and check in case they seem too pushy. It's worth taking the time to do this as it puts your business in a good light. Don't forget that job applicants are potential customers/clients too.

Checklist

✓ Think carefully about what type of advertising is most likely to reach the people you want.

✓ Decide on your advertising budget and assess where you will get the most bang for your buck.

✓ Think creatively about ways you could spread the word about your vacancy (local community magazines, noticeboards, etc).

✓ If you are using a recruitment agency, make sure they are reputable and check the terms and conditions of your contract carefully.

✓ Check your advert thoroughly to make sure that there are no embarrassing mistakes that will reflect badly on your business.

✓ Think carefully about the messages you want to get across in your job advert and allow enough time to write it up in an appealing and informative way.

✓ Make sure your advert complies with equality legislation.

CHAPTER 6
Getting ready to interview

📖 What's in this chapter?

From shortlisting candidates to asking the right kinds of questions at interviews, you need to prepare yourself thoroughly for the selection process. After all, you can't really afford to make the wrong decision. What's more, you need to make sure you don't fall foul of the law.

In this chapter we'll cover:

→ deciding which applications to pursue and which to reject

→ thinking through the logistics of the interview process

→ whether it would be useful to ask the candidate to make a presentation or take a test

→ making a list of questions you'd like to ask — and becoming aware of those questions you need to avoid

→ gaining an understanding of the different types of questioning technique and how to use them

→ how to take a logical and informed approach to deciding who is the best person for the job.

Shortlisting

So you've had a good response to your advert and the applications are rolling in. You now need to decide which candidates you would like to call in for an interview.

If you've had an overwhelming number of applicants, it can be difficult to choose who to see. The following questions will help you decide which applications you'd like to pursue further.

-> How much time are you prepared to set aside to interview candidates? If you want to spend a day, for example, you probably couldn't realistically do a thorough interview with more than four or five people. Don't forget you will need time to prepare and make notes between interviews.

-> How well do the applicants compare against your job description and person specification? (See p. 48.)

-> Are there people who don't have any of the basic skills you need for the job? If so, you can put these on the "no" pile straight away.

-> How many of the candidates have the skills and experience you rated as essential to do the job?

-> If you still have too many people who claim to have essential skills, how many of them also have some of desirable skills?

-> Could you benefit from a second eye? You need to treat applications confidentially, but if you are involving someone else in the recruitment process, it's worth getting them to look through the forms or CVs too.

Once you've whittled down the applications, you can then invite the potential candidates in for an interview. It's probably wise at this stage not to reject any candidates you aren't inviting in – you may need to go to your "reserve" list if you don't find the right person first time round.

Make sure the letter or email you send gives the following information:

-> the time and location of the interview (provide a map or directions if possible), including where they should report to on arrival

-> the names of the people who will interview the candidates

-> how long you expect the interview to take

-> if appropriate, what format the interview will take (for example, whether they will be required to make a presentation or take any kind of test).

You also need to ask candidates if they have any special needs that you will need to cater for.

It's a good idea to ask people to confirm that they will be attending – that way, if anyone decides not to come along, you can invite someone from your "reserve" list.

Preparing for the interview

Small businesses are always under pressure. If you've taken the decision to hire, it probably means you're already doing the job of two (if not more) people. If you're juggling lots of conflicting priorities, you might feel you can't spare the time to think too much beforehand about how you are actually going to conduct the interview.

Take a step back and think about this for a minute, though. Deciding to employ someone is potentially one of the most important decisions you will make for your business. The right candidate could make a huge difference to the future success of your venture. Take on the wrong person, however, and it could cost you dearly – in stress and anxiety, not to mention the time and resources needed to start the whole recruitment process all over again. The old adage "fail to prepare, prepare to fail" really rings true in this scenario. Setting time aside to plan how you are going to manage the interview will definitely pay dividends.

Don't forget that an interview is a two-way process – you want to find out about the candidate, but they also want to find out about you and whether they want to work for your business.

If you approach the interview in a professional manner, it will present your business in a good light – and go a long way towards ensuring you make the right decision.

Key issues

Below are some of the issues to think about when you're preparing for an interview.

Where will the interview be held?

You need to identify a quiet space where you can conduct the interview privately and without interruptions. Think about how to arrange the seating. Ideally, you want people to relax, so try not to make it feel too formal. An interview is a nerve-racking process for candidates at the best of times – and if you're sitting behind a big formal desk or on a chair that's higher than theirs it will immediately make people feel apprehensive and uncomfortable. Make sure there's a jug of water on hand too.

Do you want the candidate to make a presentation?

This is quite common for managerial roles. It's a good opportunity to see how the applicant performs on their feet, gives an indication of how they approach tasks, and can also showcase their creativity or research skills.

You might want a potential sales manager, for example, to outline how he or she would approach a new market, or a PR manager to describe how they would tackle publicity for a product launch. If you decide to go down this route, make sure you provide a clear brief and state how long you have allocated for the presentation, how you would like it delivered (eg informal or PowerPoint) and whether any necessary equipment will be available.

Do you want the candidate to take any kind of test?

If you are recruiting for a technical or admin-type role, you might want to consider asking candidates to take an appropriate test. A hairdressing salon, for example, might ask a potential recruit to cut the hair of a volunteer model, so the manager can make a judgement about how well they wield the scissors and see their customer relationship skills in action. It's quite common for job-seekers applying for secretarial roles to be asked to demonstrate their word processing skills or for a potential receptionist to showcase their telephone skills.

If you decide to administer this kind of test, make sure it is appropriate to the job in hand, achievable in the time you have set, and that all candidates are asked to jump through exactly the same hoops!

Psychometric tests are sometimes used when recruiting more senior staff. These tests can help to give recruiters insights into a candidate's personality type or their aptitude in specific areas such as decision making or problem solving. They can help you build up a picture of a potential candidate, but they can't guarantee how well someone will perform in a particular role. They can be a useful part of the recruitment process, but shouldn't be the main factor on which you base your final decision.

> **Startups Tip**
> Psychometrics is not a job for the amateur – if you want to use this kind of assessment tool you will need to bring a qualified practitioner in to conduct them for you.

What questions do you need to ask?

You will need to prepare at least a basic list of questions in advance of the interview. This will ensure that you:

⇢ cover all the necessary issues and don't forget to ask something vital

⇢ cover the same areas with all candidates so that you can make a sensible comparison

⇢ make the best use of the time available to you.

Of course, this doesn't mean you have to stick laboriously to a pre-prepared list of questions – sometimes the conversation will give rise to a question you hadn't thought about beforehand or will highlight an area you'd like to pursue further with a promising candidate. A list of questions will, however, help you keep the interview on track and make sure that by the time the candidate leaves you have gathered all the information you need to help you make a decision.

We talk more about specific types of interview questions – and the questions you can't ask – in the section on the interview process below.

What style and tone do you want to set?

Do you want the interview to be an informal chat or a more formal affair? How structured or unstructured do you want it to be?

Are you going to conduct the interview solo or with a colleague?

Two pairs of hands (or in this case, ears and eyes) are often better than one, and it's certainly worth considering getting someone else to help you with the interview process.

A second person can make more detailed notes while you are asking the questions, so that you can concentrate on engaging with the candidate and listening to what they have to say. They may also pick up on body language or nuances that you have overlooked.

If you are recruiting your first member of staff, you might want to ask a trusted friend or fellow professional to sit in with you. If you already have staff on board, it would certainly make sense to include someone who will be their manager or who they will work alongside. You could also engage the services of an independent HR professional to help you with the recruitment process.

Think beforehand about how the two of you will split the interview process. Who will start and who will close the interview? Who will ask which questions or cover which topics? At which point will you hand over to each other?

The interview process

Try to go into the interview with an open mind. It's easy to be swayed by a particularly persuasive CV before you've even met the person, or to have developed favourable feelings towards a particular candidate because they come highly recommended by someone you know. People are not always who they seem to be on paper – and your opinion of what makes a good employee may not be the same as someone else's – so it's best to start with a blank page.

It's a good idea to have a clear structure in mind for the interview so that you can keep to time and ensure you have covered all the key points. Make sure you:

-▷   welcome the candidate and try to put them at their ease

-▷   introduce yourself and anyone else involved in the interview process

-▷   tell them what to expect, ie what form the interview will take and how long it will last

-▷   give some basic details up front about the business, the role you are recruiting for and how it fits into the overall picture

-▷   cover all the questions you have planned in advance

-▷   give the candidate time to clarify information and ask any questions they may have

-▷   tell people what will happen next and when, ie if there is going to be a second round of interviews or a further test, and when they can expect to hear back from you.

If you can, take notes during the interview, but keep them brief or you will interrupt the flow of the conversation. Make sure you have scheduled enough time between interviews to write up your thoughts and impressions about each candidate more fully, or you may have forgotten them by the time you get to the end of a long day.

What to ask . . .

You should already have thought about the information you need to elicit from potential employees, but it's worth spending a bit of time thinking about how you will actually ask the questions.

If you're new to interviewing, it's tempting to fall back on the kinds of questions you've probably been asked a million times yourself in job interviews. Here are some typical questions.

-▷   Tell us about your current job.

-▷   What are your main duties and responsibilities?

-▷   Why do you want to leave?

-> What attracts you to this role?

-> What are your strengths and weaknesses?

-> Where do you see yourself in five years' time?

These are all perfectly valid, open questions that allow the candidate to talk freely about their experience and aspirations. They will give you the opportunity to form an impression of the person and to gather information about their career history. These kinds of question won't, however, necessarily give you an indication of how well the individual is likely to perform in the role you are recruiting for.

In other words, they will tell you what the person has done in their career to date, but they won't tell you how well (or otherwise) they did it, or what they might be capable of doing in the future.

Competency-based questions can be a useful way of digging a bit deeper and getting a more accurate picture of a candidate's ability and potential. They can give you an indication of how someone prefers to work and how they might behave if they were confronted with a particular type of situation or challenge. It's estimated that around a third of all employers now use what are known as competency (or behavioural) interviews when they are recruiting people.

Competency-based questions

The competencies you require will vary according to the job in question. Typically, though, competencies are skills in areas like team-building, leadership, delegation, communication, creativity, influencing and risk-taking, to name just a few. You can try to judge a candidate's level of ability in a particular competency by asking them questions about how they have used these skills to good effect in the past.

So if you wanted to test someone's ability to communicate well, for example, you might ask them:

-> to describe a time when they had to win over someone who was reluctant or unresponsive

-> to demonstrate how they vary their communication approach according to the audience

↝ to give an example of when their communication skills made a difference to a situation.

You might also use this approach if you wanted to test someone's ability to be creative and innovative. You could, for example, ask them to describe a time when they felt a conventional approach would not be suitable. How did they devise and manage a new approach? What challenges did they face and how did they address them?

Below are some examples of competency-based questions you could use when trying to judge someone's ability to make decisions.

↝ Tell us about a time when you had to make a decision without knowledge of the full facts.

↝ Describe a decision you made that you knew would be unpopular with a group of people. How did you handle the decision-making process and how did you manage expectations?

↝ Give an example of a situation where you had to make a decision without the input of key people – for example when a manager was unavailable at the critical time.

Examples of questions courtesy of Interview Skills Consulting Ltd, www.interview-skills.co.uk

You may decide to base your interview solely around these kind of competency-based questions, or to use a mix of approaches.

Whichever route you decide to follow, make sure you don't ask closed questions (ie questions that only allow the candidate to respond with "yes" or "no") and that you take the opportunity to probe any areas that give you cause for concern.

There may, for example, be a gap in someone's CV that you'd like to investigate further, or a candidate may tell you something that doesn't quite add up. There may be a perfectly reasonable explanation, but this is your chance to find out.

You have no doubt heard about some of the strange things candidates can be asked to do at job interviews – indeed you may have experienced some bizarre tests and challenges yourself. Andrew

Fitzimmons of Buffalo Communications remembers one particularly strange job interview. "A number of years ago, I was asked to do 40 push-ups to see if I was 'fit for the job'," he says. "The employer, a renowned car dealership, was deadly serious."

Asking candidates to do something strange may demonstrate how they react in unexpected situations, but often it just places unnecessary pressure on them. Before you begin wowing candidates with your creativity, ask yourself if weird challenges or questions actually serve a purpose.

Don't forget that it's not just the candidate who needs to make a good impression. The interview is also the potential recruit's opportunity to form an impression of the business and decide whether they would like to work for you.

We hear some strange things, such as asking candidates which animal – or even kitchen utensil – they'd be and why. Someone even had to present ideas for the business while standing on the meeting room table. I don't know how useful these are, but I doubt any of them are relevant to the job the candidate was being interviewed for.

James Callander, Managing Director of recruitment consultancy Freshminds Talent

What not to ask . . .

Once again, you need to be mindful of the legalities of the interview process. You have to make sure you are not asking questions that could lead to allegations of discrimination. There is often a thin line between what would be deemed acceptable and unacceptable questions. The following are some key areas where you need to exercise caution.

→ **Sex.** It goes without saying that you should avoid sexist comments, but you also have to be careful about asking questions about people's marital status or family intentions. So you can't, for example, ask a candidate questions such as "Are you planning to start a family?" or "What childcare arrangements do you have in place?" It is also not appropriate to ask about their marital status.

➔ **Race.** You will want to reassure yourself that someone is eligible to work in the UK, but you don't need to ask where the person's parents were born, for example. This is the kind of question that could be deemed unnecessary and potentially racist.

➔ **Disability.** Any questions relating to disability should be carefully worded. They need to centre on how you could enable a candidate with a disability to do the job rather than why their disability would exclude them.

➔ **Health.** You can't ask candidates to complete a medical questionnaire before being offered a job, and you can only discuss essential medical issues at the interview stage. Any particular physical or medical requirement should already have been made clear up front in the job advertisement.

➔ **Age.** You can enquire about someone's age in order to ascertain that they are old enough to perform the job being advertised, if it is an occupation where age discrimination is permitted (eg a driving instructor). In most cases, however, it would be deemed inappropriate to ask a candidate how old they are.

> ## Startups Tip
> Only ask questions which will help you make a decision about whether to appoint a candidate to the job. You don't need to know whether someone is married, single or divorced to decide if they are right for the role.

Hopefully, you will never find yourself in a situation where someone decides to take legal action against you on the grounds of discrimination. If you handle the recruitment process in a professional manner and pay due attention to the law, you will lessen the chances of this happening – and you will also be in a position to defend yourself if you become subject to a bogus discriminatory claim by an unscrupulous candidate looking for compensation. These cases are rare, but they do happen.

You need to be aware that if someone does make a complaint against you, they have the right to ask for copies of any notes made during the interview. It's good practice to keep a detailed record of your interview procedure and the way the decision was made so that you can use the documentation in your defence.

You shouldn't, however, keep detailed personal data about interviewees after the recruitment process is over unless it's absolutely necessary. If you do, you must make sure the data is kept securely and only used in compliance with the Data Protection Act.

To find out more about data protection in relation to employment, download the "Quick Guide to the Employment Practices Code" from the Information Commissioner's Office (ICO): www.ico.gov.uk/for_ organisations/data_protection/topic_guides/employment.aspx.

Making the decision

So the interviews are over and you are faced with making the final decision about who to recruit. If you're lucky, it will be quite straightforward. One particular candidate has stood out head and shoulders above the rest and it's clear who is the best person for the job.

It doesn't always happen like that, however. You may be faced with several candidates, all of whom are equally capable, and you're not quite sure which one to go for. Or, if you have been interviewing alongside a colleague, you may not be in agreement over who should be appointed. If you're faced with this scenario, try to be objective. Look back at the notes you have made, the results of any tests you have used, and the experience and skills the candidates have at their disposal.

If you have been consistent in the way you have interviewed people, you might want to consider using some kind of scoring system to see how the individuals stack up against each other. It's wise to do this as soon as possible after the interviews. "A lot of the subtlety and insight you've established is lost and forgotten by the time you write it up or discuss it with other assessors and stakeholders," says James Callander, Managing Director of recruitment consultancy Freshminds Talent.

Make sure you are not being swayed by first impressions or personal prejudices. You may, for example, have felt a natural affinity with a candidate – but that doesn't necessarily make them the right person for the role. Equally, you may have interviewed a candidate who, for whatever reason, is not the "type" of person you were expecting to employ, but who could clearly do a great job.

Try to approach the decision with a completely open mind – and be wary of recruiting someone who is "just like you". It's tempting to do this, because you know you will get on and work well together. That is undoubtedly an important factor – especially if they are your first employee and you will be working directly with them.

Remember, however, that if someone is "just like you" they will probably also have been blessed with your weaknesses as well as your strengths. If you're someone who's great at seeing the big picture but is not so good on detail, for example, it would probably be worth considering someone who is better than you at "crossing the t's and dotting the i's".

If you already have a team on board, it can be particularly useful to look for someone with complementary strengths. If your team is full of people who are highly creative but not particularly practical, for example, you wouldn't want to recruit someone who was just the same. The dynamics of the team and the combination of personalities, however, is important and does have to be considered.

 In my experience

Jenny Smith, Harlowsave Credit Union

Harlowsave Credit Union is a co-operative set up to provide straightforward, affordable and accessible finance to people living and working in the Harlow area. It has five staff members, including an apprentice, plus a large community of volunteers.

Manager Jenny Smith says that in her experience, a scientific approach to shortlisting and interviewing pays the best dividends.

"I look at how people have answered the application form against the criteria we have set and then do a simple 1–5 scoring to see how well they meet that and to help find the top 10 applicants," she says. "At the interview, I also score and make notes – but we don't look at the scores straight away, we chat first about each candidate and then look at the scores to see if our subjective feel matches the more objective evaluation.

"My experience is that the people who score most highly are generally the ones who turn out to be the most suitable at interview – so there is definitely something to be said for doing it that way."

The co-operative has also occasionally used tests as part of the interview process for jobs where a certain level of technical skill is required. "We have asked people to do a simple Excel spreadsheet, for example, and we also once used a basic numeracy test that had been featured in one of the tabloid newspapers, just to try to make it a fun exercise," Jenny explains.

She believes that a light, not too formal approach to the interview helps candidates show themselves in their best light. "We don't want it to be like an interrogation, so we try and make it as relaxed as possible. Our intention is to get the communication going, warm the candidate up and give them a chance to speak and tell us about themselves without nerves getting in the way."

It's important to recognise that a diverse approach to recruitment can pay real dividends in terms of the future growth and development of your business. People of different ages and from various backgrounds will all bring their unique strengths and qualities to the job, and may even help you access markets you hadn't thought about before.

It is unrealistic to suggest that your "gut feeling" isn't going to play a part in the final decision – just make sure you also take the facts into account and are not overly influenced by your instincts.

Above all, if you don't find the right person, don't panic and make an appointment that you know isn't going to work. If you can't find anyone who isn't good enough the first time around, keep looking. If you are really desperate, you can always appoint someone on a short-term contract or employ an interim or temp.

 In my experience

Daryon Eldridge, Eldridge People Solutions

Daryon Eldridge is an independent HR consultant who specialises in helping small businesses recruit and manage staff successfully. She believes interviewing "using your gut" is one of the key issues behind many bad recruitment decisions.

"The main problem with small businesses is that when they are recruiting they are often very ad hoc and don't have any process or structure to follow – or even a proper list of questions. They tend to go for the likeability factor and team fit rather than looking for strong evidence of past performance. The problem with using your gut, however, is that there are some people who are very convincing interviewees and are good at getting jobs – but not necessarily quite so good when it comes to doing the work."

Daryon cites the example of a small business who called her in after every recruitment decision they made over a year ended in disaster. A new sales manager and a key accounts person both left after only a few months in the job, which meant the company's directors had to pick up the pieces.

"It was a huge drain on senior management resources and had a knock-on effect on sales and profitability," she explains. "The crux of the problem was that they were recruiting people on the basis that they seemed nice and they thought they would fit in."

Daryon points out that failing to prepare properly for recruitment isn't just costly when people leave after only a short time in the job. "The business can end up having to dismiss someone – which they often don't handle well either – or they have to live with continued poor performance because they don't have the skills to manage the person out. They get themselves in a right pickle and it can end up costing them dearly."

She advises that if businesses do decide to call in external expertise, they need to give the HR consultant time to get to grips with the business and develop a real understanding of the role that is being recruited for. Getting professional help with drawing up a job description, with putting together an interview process, and even having a consultant sitting in on the interviews can help the business avoid disastrous mistakes.

"The key for a small business is balancing team fit with making sure you have got a person who can actually do the job and hit the ground running, because if you haven't got the resources to give them a lot of support and training you are in trouble," says Daryon.

 Checklist

☑ Put together a simple scoring system that will help you shortlist applicants for interview.

☑ Make sure you devote enough time to prepare thoroughly for the interview – decide where you will hold it, who will be involved, and how you will structure the discussion.

☑ Prepare a thorough brief for any tests or presentations you want candidates to take as part of the interview process. Remember, you need to get everyone to jump through the same hoops.

Checklist

☑ Think carefully about the questions you need to ask.
Make sure you include some competency-based questions,
which will give candidates the opportunity to demonstrate
how they have applied their skills and expertise in
the past.

☑ Gen up on equalities legislation and make sure your
interview questions comply with the rules.

☑ Consider all the evidence when making your final decision
about who to recruit. Try not to be entirely led by your
gut feelings.

☑ Don't be rushed into making a decision. Don't take
someone on for the sake of it if you are not sure they are
the right person.

CHAPTER 7

Making the appointment

 What's in this chapter?

Before making a formal job offer, you need to do some pre-employment checks – to make sure people are eligible to take up the job and are appropriate for the type of work you are offering them. But what are the key actions you need to take before getting your new recruit up and running in their role?

In this chapter we'll cover:

→ *understanding your legal obligation to conduct certain pre-employment checks*

→ *making sure the checks you conduct are not discriminatory*

→ *getting up to date on how to carry out an identity check*

→ *learning about the correct procedure for establishing whether someone has a right to work in the UK*

→ understanding the specific checks you need to make if you are employing people to work with children or vulnerable adults

→ when and how you need to check an applicant's criminal record

→ the latest thinking on taking up references

→ understanding the rules regarding pre-employment health checks

→ ensuring you are aware of your data protection duties.

Pre-employment checks are a crucial stage in the recruitment and selection process. Although some of these checks are optional, you would be well-advised to do them. They might include checking that a prospective employee does actually possess the qualifications they claim to have, or taking up references.

Other checks are a legal requirement. You have a legal obligation, for example, to make sure that an employee has a right to work in the UK. You are also required by law to obtain a Criminal Records Bureau (CRB) check on people who will be working with children or vulnerable adults, or in the security industry.

If you're under pressure it's tempting to do as little as possible, but pre-employment checks are an important part of the recruitment process. They will ensure that you are complying with the law – and also that you are recruiting someone who is suitable and appropriate for the job in hand.

The type of pre-employment checks you might want to consider include those relating to:

-> identity

-> the right to work in the UK

-> people working with children or vulnerable adults

-> CRB

-> references

-> qualifications

-> health.

You don't have to wait until all these checks are complete before telling a candidate that you would like to hire them. You can make a conditional job offer pending the outcome of the checks you have decided, or are required, to make. A conditional job offer is not a binding employment contract, and it can be withdrawn if any of the checks you've been conducting don't pan out.

Just one word of caution – you do need to make sure that your checks are not discriminatory. It would be inappropriate, for example, to conduct a health check if it wasn't necessary for the job in question, as this might discriminate against a disabled candidate.

Identity checks

The first thing you will want to check is whether the individual is who they say they are.

You can do this by asking to see an original copy of a document such as a passport, birth certificate or driving licence. If you want to make sure the prospective employee lives at the address they have given you, you can ask to see a document, such as a recent bank statement or utility bill, which has their name and address on it.

This should be sufficient in most cases, but if for any reason you are concerned you can check with the Passport Validation Service (PVS). Once you've registered with the PVS, you can access a telephone service which will help you ensure that the passport is genuine, up to date, and hasn't been reported lost or stolen. For further information, email PVS@ips.gsi.gov.uk.

Right to work in the UK

There have been enough high-profile cases splashed across the newspapers recently to make most of us aware that it's important to ensure that prospective employees from outside the UK are legally entitled to work here. There are significant penalties if an employer does not check the eligibility of an employee to work in the UK. Under the Immigration, Asylum and Nationality Act, employers who unknowingly employ an illegal worker face a maximum fine of £10,000. Those who knowingly do so could be imprisoned for two years and face an unlimited fine.

It is a complicated area, but there is plenty of help and advice out there – and the onus is on you to do your best to ascertain a prospective employee's eligibility. The current advice from the UK Border Agency is that you should both ask to see an individual's passport and also check that they have an appropriate and up-to-date visa which makes them eligible for work.

Since early 2012, checking whether foreign nationals do have a right to work in the UK has become much easier, thanks to the introduction of biometric residence permits. These are credit card-sized immigration documents that hold a person's fingerprints and photograph on a secure chip. The UK Border Agency plans to issue these permits to all migrants from outside the EEA who successfully apply to stay in the UK for more than six months. They will replace the myriad of documents UK employers currently have to use, and will provide one standard, recognisable and secure document for companies to check. Since spring 2012, it has been possible for employers to verify applicants' details via a new online checking service. More information is available from www.ukba.homeoffice.gov.uk/business-sponsors/preventing-illegal-working.

> ### *Startups Tip*
> Read the CIPD's fact sheet on employing overseas workers to get guidance on which overseas nationals are free to enter and work in the UK (www.cipd.co.uk/hr-resources/factsheets).

Those entitled to work in the UK

In terms of their freedom to enter the UK and work, there are several broad categories of overseas nationals.

-> Those who are free to enter, remain and work in the UK with minimal restriction on their length of stay or ability to enter or change employment include nationals of the "old" European Economic Area (EEA) countries, Swiss nationals and nationals of other countries who have been granted indefinite leave to remain. The "old" EEA countries other than the UK are: Austria, Belgium, Denmark, Finland, France, Germany, Greece, Iceland, Ireland, Italy, Liechtenstein, Luxembourg, Netherlands, Norway, Portugal, Spain and Sweden.

-> Those with greater, but still limited, restrictions on their ability to enter and work in the UK include nationals of the Accession 8 (A8) countries that joined the EU in May 2004 (Czech Republic, Estonia, Hungary, Latvia, Lithuania, Poland, Slovakia and Slovenia), who need to register under the Accession Worker Registration

Scheme; Commonwealth nationals with UK ancestry; and dependents of British citizens and EEA nationals. (Cyprus and Malta also joined the EU in 2004, but their nationals are not included in the Worker Registration Scheme.)

→ Those from Bulgaria or Romania (these countries joined the EU on 1 January 2007), often referred to as "A2" nations, who still need permits or equivalent to take up employment in the UK.

→ Those admitted to the UK with temporary permission as students or participants in short-term employment, including exchange schemes, or for training or work experience.

→ Those admitted to work in the UK in certain sectors on a "permit-free basis" but who still require specific and time-limited permission.

→ Those requiring full employment-based permission to work in the UK.

Once you have ascertained which category the prospective employee falls into, you need to check the relevant documents. It is vital to retain proof of the documents checked, so that you can show you have exercised due diligence in the event of any problem.

As you can see from the above, visa and permit requirements vary depending on which category an individual is in. The variations are too numerous and complex to outline in detail here, but there is a wealth of information about specific circumstances on the UK Border Agency website: www.ukba.homeoffice.gov.uk. The agency also has an employers' helpline: 0300 123 4699.

Onus of responsibility

Despite saying that she had "never knowingly employed an illegal immigrant", Baroness Scotland was fined £5,000 in 2009 for employing a housekeeper who was not legally entitled to work in the UK. She was the Attorney General at the time, and the revelation caused a great deal of embarrassment to the Brown government.

Checks for those working with vulnerable groups, including children

The new Disclosure and Barring Service (DBS) has been set up to manage the checking process that is required for some people working with children and adults. The new organisation was created through the merger, in December 2012, of the Independent Safeguarding Authority (ISA) and the Criminal Records Bureau (CRB)

The DBS

Part of the DBS's role is to help prevent unsuitable people from working with vulnerable groups, including children. It assesses individuals working or wishing to work in regulated activity to make sure they do not pose any possible risk of harm to vulnerable groups.

It's a bit of a work in progress and, at the time of writing, changes are still being made to the way the scheme operates.

Employers do, however, have certain responsibilities under the scheme and need to be aware of the law regarding employees who may be working with vulnerable groups, including children. The rules apply to a wider range of activities than you might expect, so it's important to think about the kind of work you do and whether this is an area of legislation you need to comply with.

The DBS states the following:

- A person who is barred from working with vulnerable groups, including children, will be breaking the law if they work or volunteer, or try to work or volunteer, with those groups.
- An organisation which knowingly employs someone who is barred to work with those groups will also be breaking the law.
- If your organisation works with vulnerable groups and you dismiss or remove a member of staff or a volunteer because they have harmed a child or vulnerable adult, you must tell the DBS.

Penalties are severe.

Employers recruiting new staff or volunteers must undertake an additional pre-employment check if the individual will be working in what is called "regulated" activity. If you deal with vulnerable groups, you must check a person's DBS status before employing them. You cannot take their word for it, and neither can you allow them to work in a regulated activity – even if they are supervised – before you know the outcome of the check. This doesn't just apply to employers in the traditional care and education sectors, because the definitions of "child", "vulnerable adult" and "regulated activity" are so wide (we talk more about these definitions on p. 107.) Employees such as school bus drivers and dentists will also be affected.

When the scheme is fully up and running, each individual employee or volunteer will carry a portable DBS certificate, and a potential employer, prior to altering a job, will be able to undertake an online check to see if that individual has a valid certificate.

What is regulated activity?

Getting to grips with the "regulated activities" definition is key to understanding whether your business, or certain activities within it, are affected by the DBS. You need to think about your work activities to see if any job role might fall within the definition of "regulated activities".

Regulated activity is any activity that involves contact with vulnerable groups, including children. This could be paid or voluntary work. Before looking at the type of work involved, we need to understand the definition of "child" and "vulnerable group". A child is a person aged under 18. In a workplace context, this does not include 16- and 17-year-olds. The term "vulnerable adult" is no longer used as it was considered inappropriate to label some as such based solely on their age, circumstances or disability. In general terms, an adult is now considered vulnerable if they:

→ are living in residential accommodation (care home or special home)

→ are living in sheltered housing

→ are receiving domiciliary care in their own homes

→ are receiving any form of health care

→ require assistance in the conduct of their own affairs.

This definition is not limited to the frail, elderly or infirm. Any adult can potentially be a "vulnerable" adult. Their vulnerability depends on the situation they are placed in at a particular time. A good example is an individual who visits a dentist. That individual is a "vulnerable adult" when they are undergoing examination or treatment, but not in other circumstances.

According to the ISA, regulated activity includes:

→ any activity of a *specified nature* (see below) that involves contact with vulnerable groups within a certain period, or overnight

→ any activity allowing contact with vulnerable groups that is in a *specified place* (see below), frequently or intensively.

Specified activities are:

→ teaching

→ training

→ care

→ supervision

→ advice

→ treatment

→ transportation.

Specified places are:

→ schools

→ care homes

-◇ nurseries

-◇ hospitals

-◇ prisons

-◇ detention centres.

It is without doubt a complex area and the key advice is – if in doubt, ask! A lot of help and guidance is available from the DBS website (www.homeoffice.gov.uk/agencies-public-bodies/dbs).

Criminal record checks

It is estimated that a fifth of the working population has a criminal record. It's unlikely, however, that an applicant with a criminal record will tell you about it unless they are specifically asked.

Research suggests that it is at least eight times harder for a person with a criminal record to get a job, and candidates know that it will jeopardise their chances if they reveal details about an unsavoury past. There's no doubt that the existence of a criminal record deters many employers – although it does of course depend on the nature of the offence.

It is perfectly acceptable to ask someone to disclose whether they have a criminal record if you are about to make them a job offer. In most cases, you will have to trust that a candidate has answered the question truthfully. An applicant is, however, perfectly entitled to answer "no" to the question if they do have a record but their conviction is regarded as "spent". Under the Rehabilitation of Offenders Act 1974, any conviction for a criminal offence can be regarded as spent if:

-◇ the conviction did not carry a sentence excluded from the Act (ie a custodial sentence of over two and a half years)

-◇ no further convictions occurred within the rehabilitation period.

There are exceptions to this. Certain occupations, for example, are excepted (see information below), and custodial sentences of over two and a half years are never considered spent.

The law states that there are certain circumstances in which you are obliged – or would want – to check an applicant's criminal record. For certain jobs and professions, an employer is legally obliged to perform a criminal record check before taking someone on. This check is also carried out by the DBS.

As you would expect, the list includes jobs that involve working with vulnerable groups (see previous information on "regulated activities", p. 106). The list of jobs and professions that are eligible for DBS checks is, however, quite wide. Basically, you are entitled to check a job applicant's criminal record if the role you are recruiting for is exempt from the Rehabilitation of Offenders Act 1974.

The DBS provides a system of background checks on employees and volunteers; there are three types of check currently in operation. The Gov.UK website describes these as being as follows:

1. A *standard check* contains spent and unspent convictions, cautions, reprimands and final warnings.

2. An *enhanced check* is as above plus any additional information held locally by police forces that is considered relevant.

3. An *enhanced with lists check* is as above but also includes a check with the DBS barred lists.

Generally, any position that involves working with vulnerable groups requires an enhanced disclosure.

See www.gov.uk/crb-criminal-records-check or Disclosure Scotland (www.disclosurescotland.co.uk) for more information.

Taking up references

There is no legal onus on you to take up references on a candidate you are considering hiring. It is, however, common practice and can provide added reassurance that you have made the right decision.

It's usual to ask a candidate to give the names of two or three potential referees that you can approach. Under normal circumstances, you would want to seek references from their most recent employer, but if you are recruiting someone in their first job or who has had a long career break, this may not be possible. In this scenario, alternative referees might be someone the candidate has worked with in a voluntary capacity, a college or university tutor, or someone in the community who can give them a character reference. Bear in mind, though, that personal referees have been chosen by the candidate and are unlikely to give an unfavourable picture!

You need to ask a candidate's permission when you are intending to take up a reference with their current employer. Bear in mind that their current company may not be aware that they are looking to change jobs, so this needs to be handled with some sensitivity. It is quite common – and indeed acceptable – for a candidate to ask that you don't take up a reference with their current employer unless a firm job offer is made.

You can make your job offer conditional on receiving a satisfactory reference. If you do this, your contract with the employee does not come into force until the reference is received. A word of caution here: if you let the employee start work *before* references have been received, the new recruit will have the same rights as any other employee – in relation to wrongful dismissal, for example (see Chapter 9).

How to seek a reference

The most common way to ask for a reference is in writing. You could provide a standard form for the previous employer to fill in, or simply ask them to write an "open" letter with the information you have asked for. Make sure you mark your request "private and confidential".

The kinds of questions you might ask could include the following.

- How long has the candidate worked for their current employer?
- What were the main responsibilities of their job?
- How much sick leave have they taken?
- How did they perform in the role? Were they reliable, honest and diligent?

⇢ Have they ever been the subject of any disciplinary action (and if so, for what)?

⇢ Are there any reasons why they should not be employed?

You need to be aware that previous employers are perfectly within their rights to refuse to give a reference. In practice, most will provide one – but you may find they are very cautious in their replies. This is because in our increasingly litigious society some companies have found themselves getting their fingers burned when disgruntled former employees have taken them to court.

It is becoming increasingly common practice for employers to give what are known as "bare minimum" references. You will find that many also put a disclaimer on the end of references to safeguard them against the possibility of future legal action, although these would not stand up in court if they have mis-stated the facts.

The CIPD advises that if former employers do provide a reference, they are obliged to provide information that is:

⇢ *fair and accurate*

⇢ *does not give a misleading overall impression of the employee*

⇢ *based on fact or capable of independent verification*

⇢ *does not include subjective information as to the applicant's suitability for the job being offered.*

If a reference gives you cause for concern – or you feel that you need further information – you can telephone the referee to seek clarification. If you do this, it's best to make an appointment for the call in advance – and you may find that some employers do not welcome this type of approach.

Be aware that employees do have the right – under certain circumstances – to ask to see references that have been written about them. The employer who supplied the reference is not legally obliged to share it, but you, as the employer receiving the reference, may well be obliged to supply a copy.

Any information you obtain about candidates during the recruitment process should be held in a way that meets the requirements of the Data Protection Act 1998 (read more about data protection in relation to pre-employment checks on p. 119). Individuals have a right to a copy of information held about them which is covered by the Act.

There are a few issues to bear in mind when considering this kind of request. Some of the information provided in a reference – such as dates of employment and number of days taken off sick – will be known already to the candidate, so there is no good reason to withhold them. They may also be well aware of details about their performance in their previous role: if it was discussed with them in an appraisal, for example.

If, however, you suspect that there are details in the reference that the candidate may not have been previously aware of – such as the referee's opinion of their capability, for example – you should contact the referee and ask if they have any objection to the information being shared. Even if they ask you to keep their reference confidential, you still need to weigh up the facts carefully, think about the interests of both parties, and decide whether it is reasonable to share the reference, even without their consent.

The Information Commissioners Office (ICO) provides the following best practice guidelines.

> In most circumstances, you should provide the information in a reference, or at least a substantial part of it, to the person it is about if they ask for it. Even if the referee refuses consent, this will not necessarily justify withholding the information, particularly where this has had a significant impact on the individual, such as preventing them from taking up a provisional job offer. However, there may be circumstances where it would not be appropriate for you to release a reference, such as where there is a realistic threat of violence or intimidation by the individual towards the referee.
>
> You should consider whether it is possible to conceal the identity of the referee, although often an individual will have a good idea who has written the reference. If it is

not reasonable in all of the circumstances to provide the information without the referee's consent, you should consider whether you can respond helpfully anyway (for example, by providing a summary of the content of the reference). This may protect the identity of the referee, while providing the individual with an overview of what the reference says about them.

You can find further details about your rights and responsibilities with regard to references on the ICO's website: www.ico.gov.uk.

Checking qualifications

You can also check whether an applicant does actually possess the qualification or level of qualification they claim to have. Your decision about whether to do this will depend on how important the qualification is in relation to the job. There are some professions, such as the medical professions, where people are not allowed to practise without the appropriate qualification. There are others, such as accountancy where a qualification is an indicator of a person's knowledge and competence.

There are a number of ways you can check a candidate's qualifications.

→ Ask to see their certificate(s) – although in reality, if people have qualified some time ago, these will probably have long been lost.

→ Check with the awarding body for the qualification.

→ Use a commercial checking service, such as Experian. This can help you check personal details as well as information about qualifications. You can find more details about how to do this via the website www.candidateverifier.com.

If you are unfamiliar with a particular qualification or unsure at what level it is pitched, the Department for Education may be able to help. Their general enquiries telephone number is 0370 000 2288.

If you need information about overseas qualifications and how they compare with equivalents in the UK, the UK National Academic Recognition Information Centre (UK NARIC) may be able to help (www.ecctis.co.uk/naric).

Health checks

In some circumstances, you may wish to carry out a health check or medical assessment to make sure a candidate is "fit" for the job in hand. You may need to make sure, for example, that they are physically strong enough to carry out the work or that their eyesight meets the standards needed for a specific role. As you will have seen earlier, you cannot ask about a candidate's health earlier in the recruitment process unless you have good reason to do so – if a certain level of physical ability is necessary for the job, for example.

A pre-employment health check could be anything from simply asking a candidate's previous employer to provide information about their sickness absence record to requesting the applicant undergo a full medical.

Some employers issue a "health questionnaire" to help them decide if a fuller investigation is needed. These questionnaires would typically contain questions about a candidate's lifestyle and their personal and family medical history. Depending on the answers, you can decide whether you want to pay for a detailed medical examination. Drawing up this kind of questionnaire is not, however, a job for the amateur, and you would be well advised to call in the services of an occupational health specialist to help you with this.

Whichever route you choose, however, this is definitely an area where you need to make absolutely sure you are not inadvertently being discriminatory. The intention of any pre-employment health screening should be to identify any risks to the candidate themselves or to the colleagues and clients they may be working with. It can also help you to identify any "reasonable adjustments" you need to make to enable a disabled candidate to do the job (see Chapter 4).

In some cases, a candidate may not be disabled, but might need some additional support or equipment to help them work successfully in the role. Someone with a history of back problems, for example, may need to sit in a particular kind of chair. In other words, the purpose of a health check should be to screen people in rather than to screen them out.

You can make a job offer conditional on the results of any tests, provided you state this clearly when you write to an applicant to offer them the post.

Gov.UK offers the following useful guidance to help you decide whether it is appropriate to carry out a pre-employment health assessment.

You should only complete pre-employment health checks:

--> where any candidate would be required to undergo testing to determine if they are fit to carry out the job

--> where testing is needed to meet legal requirements – eg eye tests for commercial vehicle drivers

--> when you are sure you need this information and are able to securely hold the information as per the Data Protection Act 1998.

Further information can be found at: www.gov.uk/employers-checks-job-applicants.

If you ask the candidate to undertake any kind of medical test or examination, you should explain clearly why it is necessary and get them to agree in writing that the results will be made available to you.

You can arrange a medical test through a GP or private medical services provider.

Be aware that applicants have the right to see any medical report and can ask for it either to be withheld from you or amended.

If a health check does suggest that the candidate would not be able to carry out all or part of the job, you will need to think carefully about whether any "reasonable adjustment" could be made to overcome this (see Chapter 4).

Social networking sites

As an employer, it's very tempting to use one of the social networking sites, such as Facebook or LinkedIn, to try to find out a bit more about a prospective candidate. It's human nature to want to dig a bit deeper and try to build more of a personal picture of the person you are seriously considering recruiting.

In the UK, there is no law at the moment to stop you from doing this, although the legal profession is beginning to look at the issue from the point of view of privacy and intrusion. It's interesting to note that in Germany, however, laws are being developed to stop employers from using sites like Facebook as a factor in selecting candidates.

It is difficult to see how this kind of law could be enforced. One of the key purposes of LinkedIn, for example, is to enable professionals to share information about their experience and expertise. Indeed, some candidates may even direct you to their LinkedIn profile as a source of further information.

It is amazing what some individuals are prepared to share on sites like Facebook, although if they are sensible (and particularly if they are job-hunting) they will have chosen a privacy setting that blocks anyone other than their "friends" from seeing embarrassing photographs of them staggering out of the pub on a Friday night.

What you need to remember, however, is that although using social network sites to aid your recruitment decisions is not illegal, it is not necessarily advisable. People often elaborate their achievements or paint an exaggerated picture of themselves on these sites. You can't take everything you read as gospel – and the fact that someone likes a few drinks at the weekend or engages in silly banter with their friends on Facebook doesn't necessarily mean they wouldn't be wholly professional at work.

So do it if you must – and you probably won't be able to help yourself – but make sure you are not placing too much emphasis on what you find when it comes to making a final recruitment decision.

Data protection issues

Information that comes into your hands during pre-employment checks can be highly sensitive. As an employer, you have an obligation to treat it confidentially and keep it securely in accordance with the Data Protection Act 1998.

There are eight data protection principles. The ICO advises that data should be:

- *processed fairly and lawfully*
- *obtained only for one or more specified and lawful purposes, and not processed in any manner incompatible with that purpose/s*
- *adequate, relevant and not excessive in relation to the purpose/s for which it is obtained*
- *accurate and, where necessary, kept up to date*
- *not kept longer than is necessary for the purpose for which it is being used*
- *processed in accordance with the rights of individuals*
- *kept secure and in a way that prevents unlawful access or processing and guards against accidental loss or destruction*
- *not transferred outside the European Economic Area, unless there is an adequate level of protection of information.*

Put simply, you should only collect information that you genuinely need, and use it only for the purposes you gathered it for in the first place. Make sure it is accurate and kept up to date and that you don't keep it any longer than necessary. Put measures in place to ensure that any information you hold as a result of pre-employment checks is only accessible to people who need it.

There are even tighter rules for the management of sensitive information that might be revealed as a result of a criminal records check, for example.

The Data Protection Act defines sensitive personal data as the following information about an individual.

→ alleged criminal activity

→ court proceedings

→ health

→ political opinions

→ racial or ethnic origin

→ religious beliefs

→ sexual life

→ trade union membership.

If you are dealing with this kind of data, there is an even greater onus on you as an employer to make sure that you are justified in gathering the information, are using it in a fair manner and are keeping it secure. There is more detailed guidance on this on the ICO's website: www. ico.org.uk.

This is an issue that needs to be treated seriously. If you are found to be in breach of the Data Protection Act, you could find yourself facing a fine. The maximum penalty for really serious breaches is £500,000.

The Information Commissioner's Office (ICO) found East and North Hertfordshire NHS Trust to be in breach of the Data Protection Act after an unencrypted USB stick containing sensitive personal data was lost on a train journey home.

The USB stick was used by a junior doctor to record brief details of patients' conditions and medication before being handed to the next doctor on shift. In this incident the doctor had taken the USB stick home intending to forward the data electronically, but lost the unprotected device on a train.

Withdrawing job offers

You may find yourself in the unfortunate position of having to withdraw a job offer because the results of a pre-employment check have not been satisfactory.

If you have made it clear that any job offer is subject to satisfactory references or a specific kind of check, this is straightforward. There is no contract between you, and you simply advise the candidate that the checks have been unsatisfactory and that the job offer is no longer on the table.

The situation is more complex if you had an urgent recruitment need and have already allowed the candidate to start work. As we have seen earlier, once a new recruit has started working for you, they have the same rights as any other employee.

Closing the recruitment process

Once your job offer has been accepted and you are sure the person you've chosen is going to come on board, you need to get back to the other applicants and let them know they have not been successful. This is a common courtesy that is overlooked by many businesses. If you've ever job-hunted yourself, you know how frustrating it is when your application disappears into the ether and you never hear a word. It really doesn't take long to send a quick letter or email to candidates thanking them for their application and letting them know that they haven't been selected for interview.

You should let the candidates you've interviewed know as soon as possible that they have not been selected. It's good practice to thank them for their time and to respond to requests for a bit of post-interview feedback if asked. It's not only common courtesy, it will also present your business in a positive and professional light and will stand you in good stead if you come into contact with candidates again, either as potential recruits or future customers.

Checklist

☑ Conduct an identity check on your chosen candidate
— you cannot assume someone is who they say they are,
however convincing they may seem.

☑ Make sure your potential recruit has the right to work in
the UK.

☑ If you are recruiting for a post that involves working with
children or vulnerable adults, make sure you conduct the
appropriate checks.

☑ Consider making your job offer conditional on the receipt
of satisfactory references.

☑ If appropriate, check that the candidate is in possession
of the relevant/necessary qualification.

☑ If appropriate, arrange for pre-employment health
screening — although you must ensure that this is not
inadvertently discriminatory.

☑ Take the time to contact unsuccessful candidates to
advise them that they have not been selected for the job.

↩ CHAPTER 8

Getting up and running with a new employee

📖 What's in this chapter?

So you've finally found the right person, they've accepted your job offer and you're ready to roll. But what are the key systems you need to put in place to get your new recruit up and running?

In this chapter we'll look at:

→ how to make an offer of employment

→ the key elements to include in a written statement of employment

→ what to do if you want to vary an employee's contract

→ the nuts and bolts of PAYE

→ the pros and cons of outsourcing payroll

→ the basic facts about sick pay

→ the ins and outs of NICs

→ your responsibilities with regard to employers' liability insurance.

There are some key actions you need to take to get up and running with a new employee.

First, you need to draw up a contract or provide a written statement that makes the terms of employment crystal clear for both you and the employee. You also need to set up a PAYE system for your business and to get to grips with your obligations to make National Insurance Contributions (NICs). Another priority will be to make sure you have the appropriate insurance arrangements in place.

This chapter aims to outline the key steps and to help you ensure you are complying with all the relevant rules.

Drawing up the contract

If you say the magic words "you're hired" and the candidate accepts, you have entered into a contract of employment. However, to avoid any misunderstandings in the future, it would be wise to put the contract in writing, particularly as your employee is entitled to a written statement setting out the terms and conditions of their employment. Under the Employment Rights Act 1966, you are obliged to give them this statement within two calendar months of starting work, but it's advisable to get it done straight away.

A contract of employment or written statement should include the following:

‑▷   company/business name

‑▷   name of the employee

‑▷   date when the employment begins

‑▷   if the job is not permanent, the period for which the employment is expected to last

‑▷   if the employment is for a fixed term, the date when it will end

‑▷   salary and any benefits

‑▷   how the salary will be paid (eg weekly or monthly)

- working hours
- holiday entitlement, including public holidays and holiday pay
- job title or a short description of the role
- place of work.

Either in the document or separately, you also need to set out the terms and conditions applying to:

- sickness absence and sick pay
- pension scheme
- length of notice the employee is required to give to terminate the contract
- details of disciplinary and grievance procedures, and who the employee should contact if they are unhappy with a decision.

Covering these latter items in the written statement can sometimes make it quite long and unwieldy. It is acceptable to refer recruits to separate documents that outline your policies on these issues, or to a staff handbook if you have one. We'll talk more about these and other employment policies in Chapter 9.

If all the required details are included in the offer letter you sent to the chosen candidate, there is no need to draw up a separate written statement, as you will have satisfied the requirements of the Employment Rights Act 1996.

Offers of employment should always be made in writing, but it's important to be aware that an oral job offer – made over the phone or at the close of an interview, for example – is as legally binding as a letter. So movie mogul Samuel Goldwyn was wrong when he said, "A verbal contract isn't worth the paper it's written on."

You should also be careful that you don't make any promises in an interview that you subsequently can't keep. If you offer someone a job with specific benefits and they accept, you can't then go home, do some sums and change the offer the next day because you've realised you can't afford it.

The Gov.UK website has some handy information on creating a written statement of employment or contract (www.gov.uk/employment-contracts-and-conditions).

If you are still unsure about any of the details, you can also get further information on contracts of employment from www.acas.org.uk.

> *Be cautious with your wording and don't promise the earth unless you're going to give it. If you offer them the job and they say "great, I'll start on Monday," that's a contractual agreement. Just because it's oral doesn't mean it's not binding.*
>
> Alexandra Davidson, partner with law firm Berwin Leighton Paisner

Varying contracts

Contracts of employment are not set in stone. They can be changed, but only with the agreement of both parties. For example, you may want to change the salary, working hours or responsibilities set out in the contract. Your employee's circumstances may have changed and they may wish to work shorter hours.

Changing a contract is a two-way street, and you need to consult with your employee and explain your reasons if you wish to change their contract of employment. Once you've agreed to the changes, you need to issue a new written statement, not later than one month after the change has taken place.

Amending the contract without the agreement of the employee would be a breach of contract and could lead to a claim of constructive dismissal. If you can't agree, you can terminate the contract, with proper notice, and offer a new contract including the revised terms, but this would amount to dismissing the employee and could lead to a case of unfair dismissal.

Acas publishes a handy guide to varying a contract of employment, available online at www.acas.org.uk.

Setting up PAYE

Most of us have received a payslip or two in our working lives and are familiar with the term PAYE (Pay As You Earn) – the system used to deduct tax and other payments from your pay, as you earn. If you dig out an old payslip, you'll see that it shows your gross pay and also your net pay, after deductions.

As an employer, it is not just your responsibility but also your legal obligation to operate PAYE on the pay you award to employees earning above the National Insurance Lower Earnings Limit (LEL), currently £107 per week. The PAYE threshold (at the time of writing) is £156 a week, until 5 April 2013 when it may be revised.

You will have to apply the PAYE system to all payments you make to your employees, including:

-> salary and wages

-> overtime

-> bonuses and commission

-> statutory sick pay, maternity, paternity and adoption payments

-> lump sum and compensation payments (eg redundancy payouts), unless they are exempt from tax

-> payments in kind, eg childcare vouchers. PAYE applies to the cash value of such items.

You must also hand out payslips at or before the time you pay your employees, whether that is weekly, fortnightly or monthly.

At the end of the tax year you must also give each employee a P60 summarising all the pay and deductions made up to 5 April, the end of the tax year. The P60 must be in paper format, but payslips may be distributed to staff in either paper or electronic format.

You will also have to complete an annual return. At the end of the tax year, you will have less than a month to submit this summary of your payroll figures for the year to HMRC. This is called the

Employer Annual Return, and most employers are required to file this information online using forms P35 and P14s.

Tax on expenses and benefits, including company cars, are also made as one-off payments at the end of the tax year. Guidance for employers on such payments is available on the HMRC website.

Getting started

Your first step as an employer is to register as such with HMRC. The HMRC website (www.hmrc.gov.uk) contains clear instructions and all the forms and information you will need to get started.

Once you have registered, you will receive a "PAYE reference" from HMRC with links to the website. You can register online or by calling 0845 607 0143. Customers with a hearing or speech impairment can textphone 0845 602 1380. The lines are open from 8am to 8pm (Monday to Friday) and from 8am to 4pm (Saturday).

Getting to grips with payroll

Keeping accurate payroll records is essential to ensure that you pay your employees the right amount at the right time and that you make all the necessary deductions. It is also a legal requirement. You have to prepare a P11 (Deductions Working Sheet) or equivalent payroll record for each employee earning above the LEL or for whom you have to operate a tax code. This record must show the employee's:

→ gross pay

→ NICs

→ tax deducted under PAYE

→ statutory sick pay, maternity, adoption and ordinary and additional statutory paternity payments during the year

→ any student loan deductions.

You could do this manually, but increasingly HMRC is demanding that returns are made online, with penalties for those who don't or can't. In any case, the software packages available will do all the calculations for you, and will even generate those all-important payslips for your employees. In addition, as long as the software system you opt for complies with HMRC requirements (and is compatible with your existing IT systems), going online will enable you to manage the operation seamlessly and cut down on paper-based filing.

Outsourcing options

If you are thinking of outsourcing the payroll task, your accountant should be able to provide this service. Alternatively, there are payroll agencies that specialise in taking this work off the hands of busy businesses.

Whichever option you go for, however, you must establish:

-> that the provider has the necessary resources to provide your growing business with the payroll services you need, both now and in the foreseeable future

-> whether they have expertise in your particular sector

-> what software systems an external provider uses, and that they are compatible with your IT system (as well as HMRC-accredited)

-> what the costs would be for setting up and running the operation, and what additional costs there might be

-> what back-up the provider has and where and how your records will be stored.

As with any service provider, you will need to draw up a service level agreement, especially in terms of meeting HMRC deadlines (where penalties apply if returns are not made on time).

Doing it yourself

Managing the payroll in house, either by yourself or by hiring a suitably qualified person, is also an option. There are tools to help you do this on the HMRC, website as well as plenty of commercial software packages on the market.

Once you have entered all your employee's details from their P45 (or P46, see below), the software will do all the necessary calculations and produce the figures you'll need at the end of the tax year.

Look for the Payroll Standard accreditation logo when you buy your payroll software to ensure that it meets HMRC's minimum standards. Without it, you could have your work cut out making online returns. A list of approved payroll software products is available on the HMRC website.

> ### Startups Tip
> When purchasing payroll software, look for the HMRC approved logo to ensure that it meets HMRC's standards.

Registering as an employer

As stated above, you will need to register for the PAYE Online for employers service, and this will need to be activated before you or your service providers can start filing forms. This process can take up to seven days, as you need to wait for HMRC to send you an activation code, which you will need before you can make any online submissions.

Preparing your payroll

Once you've decided what the gross pay will be, you will need the following information for each individual employee:

-> a tax code to work out how much income tax to deduct

-> A National Insurance category letter to work out how much NICs to deduct (HMRC allocate a letter of the alphabet to each of the various employer/employee NICs contribution rates).

You'll also need a P45 from your new recruit. A P45 shows an individual's PAYE tax code, and is a record of their earnings while they've been in a job and the amount of tax they've paid to date.

If they don't have a P45, you and your employee will need to complete a P46.

Changing tax codes

There are deadlines by which you must file these forms; at the start of each new tax year, HMRC will issue P9(T)/P9X forms notifying you of new tax codes to use for employees for the following tax year, from 6 April.

Tax bands are subject to change, but don't worry: once you have registered for the PAYE Online for employers service, HMRC will automatically send you tax code notices online, or you can sign up to their email alert service.

Like the words in the Beatles song, you may well feel that you're working for no one but the taxman ... but HMRC have made it a lot easier to pay tax since 1966. Moves are also afoot to modernise the PAYE system even further. There are plans to switch to "real-time" information in 2013. When the new system is introduced, employers will have to provide HMRC with information about employees' salaries, tax and National Insurance deductions at the time they are paid, rather than once a year. It's all linked in with the introduction of universal tax credits (scheduled for October 2013) and is part of a wider reform by the government of the social security system. The idea is to provide the Department of Work and Pensions with up-to-date information about an individual's earnings, so that tax credits can be calculated accurately and the number of cases of tax credits being overpaid and then later reclaimed will be significantly reduced.

Sick pay

Statutory sick pay (SSP) is paid to employees who meet certain qualifying conditions at the same time and in the same way as you would pay wages. You can use free SSP calculators provided by HMRC to calculate how much SSP to pay an employee and to see if you can recover any of it (www.hmrc.gov.uk). The rate of SSP is £85.85 per week as of April 2012 until 5 April 2013.

HMRC says that you can't automatically recover SSP. You can only recover any SSP you've paid in a tax month that's over and above 13% of your gross Class 1 NICs liability for that month.

If you pay your employees their normal wage when they're sick – and this is at least as much as the SSP they'd get – you don't have to operate the SSP scheme.

You must put your sickness policy in a written statement of employment (see p. 124).

Understanding NICs

National Insurance is a premium that employers and most employees pay through the PAYE system to help fund the welfare state. NICs provide a safety net of support and services to cover illness, unemployment, retirement and other benefits.

The NIC payments that individuals make build up their entitlement to these benefits. NICs are payable by employees provided they are aged 16 or over, are under state pension age, and earn above the National Insurance LEL.

Contributions are based on gross earnings and there are different classes of NIC, some of which are paid by both you and your employees and some that are just paid by you as the employer.

Employees pay:

→   Class 1 primary contributions – deducted from gross pay and paid to HMRC by you, the employer, usually on a monthly basis. Currently Class 1 NICs are payable at a rate of 12% of an employee's gross earnings above the "Earnings Threshold" (currently £107 a week). A reduced rate of 1% is paid on any earnings that are above the "Upper Earnings Limit" (currently £817 a week).

Employers pay:

-> Class 1 secondary contributions – payable at 13.8% of an employee's gross earnings over the "Earnings Threshold", usually on a monthly basis with Class 1 NIC payments.

-> Class 1A contributions – payable at the end of the tax year on any employee benefits you have provided (eg company cars, medical cover).

-> Class 1B contributions – payable at the end of the tax year if you have agreed a PAYE Settlement Agreement (PSA) with HMRC to account for tax on certain expenses payments and benefits. A PSA is a flexible scheme used to settle any PAYE tax and NICs contributions due to HMRC on three types of expenses and benefit:

1. minor items (eg a bunch of flowers for a sick employee)

2. irregular items (eg relocation expenses in excess of the £8,000 tax exemption threshold)

3. items it's impractical to operate PAYE on, or to value for P9D/P11D purposes (eg shared cars or taxi journeys that are difficult to attribute to individual employees).

You can use the National Insurance tables supplied by HMRC to calculate NICs for weekly and monthly paid employees. These tables are included in an Employer Pack: telephone the Annual Pack Orderline on 0845 7646 646 or order online at www.hmrc.gov.uk. The Employer Pack contains detailed guidance, but you can also phone the employers' helpline on 0845 714 3143.

You must include details of NIC deductions on payslips as well as on form P11 (Deductions Working Sheet) or an equivalent payroll record for each employee.

Self-employed people are responsible for their own NIC payments. There is also provision in the system for people to pay voluntary NICs if, for example, they have not made enough contributions in a year to count for the state pension or other long-term state benefits.

Potential payment holiday

HMRC is currently offering new businesses the opportunity to take an NICs payment holiday that could add up to savings of £50,000.

The regional employer NICs holiday is available to new businesses for a limited period, subject to certain conditions. Under the scheme, new businesses may be able to qualify for a reduction of up to £5,000 of the employer NICs that would normally be due for each of the first ten employees they take on. The "holiday" is available to new businesses starting up between 22 June 2010 and 5 September 2013. Location, location, location... is an important qualifier. If you are based in the southeast or London it looks as if you won't qualify. Full details about the scheme are available on the HMRC website (www. hmrc.gov.uk). Remember, it's only a holiday for those who qualify: if you don't qualify you will need to pay those Class 1 employer NICs.

Getting started

To get all the paperwork in order, your new employee will have to provide you with their National Insurance number. UK residents are automatically issued with this number at the age of 16. It's effectively a personal account number, and not only ensures that the NICs and tax that an individual pays are properly recorded but also acts as a reference number for the whole social security system.

If a new employee does not know their number, ask them to check a previous payslip, P60, or letter from HMRC or the Department of Work and Pensions.

If they still can't find their number (and it's a common problem!):

-→ they can fill in the form Your National Insurance Number at www. hmrc.gov.uk/forms/ca5403.pdf

-→ or you can fill in the form Employees' National Insurance Trace at www.hmrc.gov.uk/forms/ca6855.pdf.

You might expect your new recruit to show you their National Insurance number printed on a plastic card. However, HMRC is withdrawing these and replacing them with a letter containing the relevant information. The important thing is the number, which you will need to record on your payroll records and returns to HMRC for each employee.

Keeping records

Pay rates, payroll, sickness absence and sick pay, accidents, injuries and dangerous occurrences are the stats you need to keep for a minimum of three years and ideally for six years – the time limit for bringing any civil legal action against you.

The other legal requirement is to keep records of working hours (to comply with the Working Time Regulations), but rather than set up a separate file, you could use your existing pay records, for example, to keep track and record this information.

Gov.UK states that you can also keep staff records on:

→ training and appraisals

→ employment history – date joined, promotions, job title

→ absence – records of lateness, sickness and any other authorised or non-authorised absences

→ holidays

→ personal details – name, address, qualifications, terms and conditions of employment.

For periods of sickness absence, you need to record how long your employee is off sick (known as PIW (period of incapacity for work)); how much SSP (statutory sick pay) you paid; the dates when you didn't pay SSP and why. Records of supporting medical evidence – a doctor's or hospital note – should also be kept.

It is also a good idea to keep contact information for next of kin in case of accident or emergency.

All this information will prove useful to you in making decisions about recruitment – or redundancy – as well as assessing the performance and productivity of individuals. It will also be invaluable should any dispute with an employee arise.

Under the Data Protection Act 1998 any personal information you keep should be adequate, relevant and not excessive. Individuals have the right to receive a copy of any information you hold about them. Requests must be made in writing, by letter or email, and you can charge up to £10 for providing it. You are required to reply within 40 calendar days.

Data security is paramount. Ensure that paper records are kept under lock and key, that any electronic files are password-protected and that your IT system has robust anti-virus software and firewalls. It is also recommended that you put an audit trail into computerised systems to monitor access to records. Ensure that personal files are protected on laptops, memory sticks or any other storage devices.

In the early days, you may find a simple staff records system – keeping data on spreadsheets, backed up with paper copies of documents – is sufficient for your needs. As the business grows, however, you may want to consider a more sophisticated system. There are a number of HR software packages on the market that allow you to manage employee information more efficiently and to automate some processes. Some are geared specifically to small businesses, and can cost as little as £2 per employee per month.

Employers' liability insurance

Accidents happen, which is why employers are required by law to have minimum employers' liability compulsory insurance cover of £5 million.

Workplace slips and trips are the most common kinds of accident, followed by falls and injuries caused by moving or falling objects, says the Health and Safety Executive (HSE), which is responsible for enforcing this law.

Employers' liability compulsory insurance covers you against any claims for compensation made by an employee arising from injuries or illness caused at work or as a result of work. You must take out the policy with a Financial Services Authority (FSA) authorised insurer (see www.fsa.gov.uk).

Your insurer will provide you with a certificate of insurance, which must be prominently displayed in the workplace. Since 2008, employers have been allowed to display the certificate electronically, but you must ensure your employees can easily find it on the company intranet.

If you have no employees, are a family business employing close relations, or a public organisation, you may not need this insurance. To check whether or not you need it, download "Employers' Liability (Compulsory Insurance) Act 1969: A guide for employers" from the HSE (www.hse.gov.uk).

Health and safety figures

In 2010/11:

- 1.2 million working people suffered from a work-related illness
- 171 workers were killed at work
- 115,000 injuries were reported under the Reporting of Injuries, Diseases and Dangerous Occurrences Regulations (RIDDOR)
- 200,000 reportable injuries (requiring more than a three-day absence) occurred.
- 26.4 million working days were lost due to work-related illness, and workplace injuries and ill health (excluding cancer) cost society an estimated £14 billion (in 2009/10).

Checklist

- ☑ Draw up a contract of employment or written statement for your new employee.

- ☑ Set up your business for PAYE by registering with HMRC.

- ☑ Decide whether to manage PAYE yourself or to outsource it to your accountant or another external supplier.

- ☑ Make sure you understand your obligations to pay NICs for your employee.

- ☑ Set yourself up to keep the necessary records — on pay, sickness, accidents and injuries.

- ☑ Make sure you have the appropriate level of employers' liability insurance.

↪ *CHAPTER 9*

Putting the right policies in place

📖 What's in this chapter?

What formal policies do you need to put together when you start employing people? Which are mandatory and which discretionary? Where do you start?

In this chapter we'll cover:

- → your health and safety responsibilities and what you need to include in a health and safety policy

- → how to draw up a disciplinary procedure that makes it clear what kind of conduct and behaviour is expected

- → what procedures to follow if you need to take disciplinary action against an employee

- → how to put together a policy that gives you a framework for dealing with bullying

- → the key elements of an equality and diversity policy

→ why you might want to consider a policy on the use of company facilities

→ how to draw up a policy that protects your intellectual property

→ how to set out your stance on drugs and alcohol at work

→ how to put together a procedure for managing absence proactively.

There are some employment-related policies you need to have in place, and others that are not mandatory but which it would be advisable to have.

For example, if you have more than five employees, you must have a written health and safety policy; it is also a legal requirement to set out your disciplinary and grievance procedures. You might also, however, choose to have policies on the use of company facilities (eg the telephone and the internet) or to cover issues like copyright and handling confidential information.

Policies are important because they make it clear to everyone what is and isn't acceptable, how people are expected to behave towards each other at work and what the correct procedure is in the case of any problem or dispute. They don't have to be overly complicated documents that take hours to put together; indeed, there's an argument for making policies as straightforward and concise as possible, so that people are more likely to read them and will find them easier to understand and act on when necessary.

You need to make new recruits aware of your policies as part of your induction procedures (see Chapter 11). Policies also need to be easily accessible in case people want to refer to them, for example pinned up on a noticeboard, kept in a file that is open to everyone or posted on your intranet if you have one.

There's some guidance below to help you draw up your own policies, and you can also find further information on the CIPD, Acas and HSE websites: www.cipd.co.uk; www.acas.org.uk; www.hse.gov.uk.

If you don't feel confident enough to put a policy together yourself, you could engage the services of an independent HR consultant or a solicitor who specialises in employment law. They will have drawn up policies for small businesses before, and will be able to put together a document that suits your needs.

To start with, you will probably want to just focus on the key policies you really need to have. As your business grows, however, you will probably want to add some others to reflect your changing circumstances. At this stage, you might want to consider putting all your policies together in a handbook to give to all new recruits when they join.

Remember to keep up to date with changes in employment law so that you can update policies as necessary. You can ask your own solicitor or friendly local HR consultant to advise you on this, or you can subscribe to a commercial service that issues automatic updates.

The policies you are either required to have or would want to seriously consider are:

→ health and safety

→ disciplinary and grievance

→ absence

→ equality and diversity.

Policies you might also want to think about putting together include:

→ intellectual property

→ smoking, drugs and alcohol.

Priority policies

Health and safety

Health and safety law applies to all businesses, regardless of size. If you're in an industry such as construction, or your operations involve the use of hazardous substances, it's an issue that will already be high on your agenda; however, it's important to recognise that accidents, both major and minor, can happen in any kind of workplace, and as an employer, you are responsible for assessing risks and providing a safe working environment.

Figures show that on average over 200 people a year lose their lives at work. 150,000 non-fatal injuries are reported and an estimated two million people experience ill-health which is either caused or made worse by work.

Under the Health and Safety at Work Act 1974 you are responsible, as far as is reasonably practical, for:

–⧽ making the workplace safe and eliminating or controlling risks to health

–⧽ ensuring that any plant and machinery in your workplace is safe and that safe systems of work are set and followed

–⧽ ensuring that any articles or substances used in your business are moved, stored and used safety

–⧽ providing adequate welfare facilities, eg toilet facilities, drinking water, somewhere for staff to rest and eat meals

–⧽ giving workers the information, instruction, training and supervision necessary for their health and safety

–⧽ consulting workers on health and safety matters.

If you employ anyone, you need to display the Health and Safety Law poster (ISBN 978 0 7176 2493 5) in your workplace. Alternatively, you can give your employees a leaflet that contains the same information. It's called "Health and Safety Law: What you should know" (ISBN 978 0 7176 1702 9) and is available in packs from the HSE (www.hsedirect.com).

If you have more than five employees, you are legally obliged to have your policy set out in writing. All employers must conduct a risk assessment, but if you have more than five employees you are also obliged to record your findings.

According to the HSE, the common issues you need to consider include:

–⧽ asbestos

–⧽ display screen equipment

–⧽ electricity

–⧽ falls from a height

–⧽ fire and explosion

–⧽ hazardous substances

-> maintenance and building work

-> musculoskeletal disorders

-> noise

-> pressure systems

-> radiation

-> slips, trips and falls

-> stress

-> vibration

-> work equipment and machinery

-> workplace transport.

As you can see, there are implications for just about any business, of any size, working in any sector.

Under RIDDOR you have a legal duty to report work-related deaths, major injuries or "over three-day" injuries, work-related diseases, and dangerous occurrences (near-miss accidents) to HSE. Call the Incident Contact Centre on 0845 300 9923.

Organisations with 10 or more employees are legally required to keep an accident book, which can be purchased from the Stationery Office (www.tsoshop.co.uk).

Health and safety law is enforced by inspectors from the HSE or from your local authority. The HSE typically covers factories, farms and building sites, while the local authorities will look after offices, shops, hotel and catering and leisure facilities.

Drawing up a health and safety policy

A health and safety policy sets out the what, when and how of health and safety in your workplace, from carrying out risk assessments to ensuring staff are properly trained to do their jobs. It should also cover welfare issues from toilet facilities to stocking the first aid box. Compared to, say, the safe handling of dangerous chemicals, toilet arrangements may seem trivial, but they are important. It's not just about hygiene, it's also about the standards that people expect. In the past, tube workers have even threatened to go on strike because there were not enough toilets and tea-making facilities for workers at outlying "booking-on" stations.

The contents of your health and safety policy should reflect what you do as a business. You can probably put one together quite easily yourself, unless you operate in a specialist or particularly hazardous area, in which case you may need to call in some external expertise.

As a general rule, your policy should cover three key areas.

1. A statement about your commitment to providing a healthy and safe workplace and the specific aims and objectives of your policy.

2. Details of how you will manage health and safety and exactly who is responsible for what.

3. Information about the practical arrangements for training and details of any safety procedures which are specific to your business.

As your business grows, you will need to involve your employees in reviewing your health and safety policy and amending it where necessary to reflect your changing circumstances.

You can download a free policy template from the HSE website (www.hse.gov.uk) to help you structure your document.

Did you know . . . ?

- All employers and self-employed people have to assess risks at work.
- Employers with five or more employees should have a written health and safety policy.
- Employers with five or more employees have to record the significant findings of their risk assessment.
- Employers have a duty to involve their employees or their employees' safety representative on health and safety matters
- Employers have to provide free health and safety training or protective equipment for employees where it is needed.

An Introduction to Health and Safety, HSE (ww.hse.gov.uk).

Disciplinary procedures

If a piece of machinery breaks down, you just get it repaired or replace it. If your employee starts "playing up" – failing to meet the expected standards in their performance or conduct – it's not quite as easy to fix the problem. Most of us would rather avoid difficult conversations, but they are inevitable when you are managing people. What makes them easier to handle is having disciplinary procedures already in place, so that employees are clear what behaviours or conduct would trigger disciplinary action and what the process would be if they were invoked.

You therefore need to formulate this process, put it in writing – in your contract of employment to new employees or in a staff handbook – and follow it to the letter so that you are fair and even-handed in addressing any issues. If you do not follow your own written procedures, an employee could sue you for breach of contract.

Your written disciplinary procedures should include:

⇥ your disciplinary rules

⇥ what performance and behaviour will lead to disciplinary action

⇥ what action will be taken as a result.

Conduct

Humans being what they are, it is probably impossible to cover every possible misdeed, but your standards of conduct expected of employees should cover:

⇥ absence

⇥ bullying, discrimination and harassment

⇥ health and safety

⇥ making personal use of company equipment or resources in work time, eg telephones, photocopying, email, internet and/or specific websites such as Twitter, and instant messaging services

⇥ performance

⇥ timekeeping

... and any other particular issues that might be relevant to your business.

Behaviour

Your rules should also cover serious and deliberate acts in the workplace that would lead to instant dismissal. These might include:

- breach of confidentiality
- downloading obscene material
- fraud
- gross negligence
- incapacity due to drunkenness or drug taking
- insubordination
- theft
- violence
- wilful damage to property.

Detailed advice and guidance on dealing with disciplinary and grievance situations can be found in the Acas booklet *Discipline and Grievances at Work: The Acas guide* (www.acas.org.uk).

Informal approach

If you have concerns, don't wait until the problem gets out of hand. Talk to the employee and give them a chance to put their side of the story. There may, for example, be personal or family reasons why they are not performing to the required standard, or they may not be aware that following Lady Gaga on Twitter in work time constitutes "unacceptable behaviour".

Taking action

Where performance or behaviour is below expected standards, most companies have a three-strike rule – an oral warning followed by a first written warning and then a second and final written warning. These warnings contain details of the standards to be met and a timeframe for improvement. If these standards are not met the employee faces dismissal.

Suspension from work is usually the first step taken by an employer in a case of alleged gross misconduct while investigations are made. In such incidences, it would be advisable to seek legal advice and/or to contact Acas before taking any action.

Always ensure that your employees are familiar with the conduct and behaviours expected of them, and that they know about the rules and have access to them at work, for example on the intranet.

If you do need to invoke the procedures, you should:

-> deal with the issue fairly

-> be prompt and avoid any unnecessary delays in the process

-> be consistent

-> establish the facts of the case

-> inform the employee in writing about the issue, giving them reasonable notice of the date of the disciplinary meeting so that they can prepare their case. The employee has a right to be accompanied at any meeting where disciplinary action might be taken or a formal warning might be given.

Depending on the outcome, there are a range of steps that can be taken. For example, you may decide that no further action is necessary or that training or counselling will resolve the issue.

Alternatively, taking all factors into consideration, you may feel that dismissal is the only recourse. Ensure that you have issued first and final warnings and made it clear in those warnings that dismissal would result if the individual's conduct or performance did not improve. The warnings should be in writing, and should explain what the nature of the misconduct is and for how long the warning will remain in force.

In some instances, you may feel it is necessary to suspend an individual while investigating incidents of alleged gross misconduct, for example fraud or physical violence. It is advisable to include information about this process in your disciplinary procedures and to state whether this period of suspension would be with or without pay. There is some handy information on this on the Gov.UK website to help you follow the correct disciplinary procedures (www.gov.uk/taking-disciplinary-action). Keep a written record of any correspondence and meeting notes relating to the action.

In cases of dismissal – due to failure to meet the required standards of performance, for example – the employee is entitled to receive the notice period set out in their contract of employment terms and conditions.

You may decide to give payment in lieu of notice – effectively putting them on gardening leave – rather than make the individual work through their notice. Their employment ends on the last day of the notice period. You should always ensure that the notice period required on both sides is included in the contract of employment.

In cases of gross misconduct, dismissal is usually immediate, ie without any notice, and termination of the contract is effective from the day of dismissal.

Of course, an employee who has been dismissed may not always agree that you acted reasonably! If they feel they have been unfairly dismissed they may decide to dispute your version of events and take you to an employment tribunal. In the past, an employee would need to have had one year's continuous service before they could make a complaint to an employment tribunal. This all changed in April 2012, when the length of qualifying service for employees bringing an unfair dismissal claim rose to two years. (There is no minimum length of service required, however, before discrimination claims can be brought.) The new rule was brought in by the government to try to encourage employers and employees to resolve their differences, and to ease the pressure on the extremely over-burdened tribunal system.

It costs a business an average of £4,000 to defend themselves against each individual claim. As of February 2012, the maximum unfair dismissal compensatory award was £72,300. The legal costs and penalties are a stark reminder of how important it is to try to avoid issues escalating in the first place and to get it right when it comes to the disciplinary and grievance process. There are obviously also other hidden costs – in terms of impact on other employees, loss of productivity and stress – all of which can add up for any small business.

> *A decision to dismiss should only be taken by a manager who has the authority to do so. The employee should be informed as soon as possible of the reasons for the dismissal, the date on which the employment contract will end, the appropriate period of notice and their right of appeal.*
>
> Code of Practice 1: Disciplinary and grievance procedures (Acas)

Bullying

It's a sad truth that bullying and harassment does take place in the workplace as well as in the playground. It doesn't just occur in large organisations – it can take place in small businesses too. As your business grows, it's definitely an issue you need to keep a look out for. Your disciplinary policy will give you a framework for dealing with incidents of bullying if they occur, but some employers also put together a separate policy on this issue.

Acas defines bullying as "offensive, intimidating, malicious or insulting behaviour, an abuse or misuse of power through means intended to undermine, humiliate, denigrate or injure the recipient." They advise that a policy on bullying should:

→   be clear about what behaviour is unacceptable

→   include what steps will be taken to stop bullying (ie under the disciplinary and grievance procedure)

→   clarify the role and responsibility of managers.

There is a guide on how to deal with bullying and harassment on the Gov.UK website (www.gov.uk/workplace-bullying-and-harassment). There's also plenty of guidance available from Acas (www.acas.org.uk).

Grievance procedures

With grievance procedures, the boot is on the other foot. These procedures provide employees with the opportunity to raise concerns, problems or complaints with you.

Unlike disciplinary procedures, there are no legally binding processes that need to be followed. Issues that might arise include disagreements with co-workers, discrimination, disputes about pay and working conditions, terms of employment and statutory employment rights.

Keeping an "open door" policy means that your employees should feel able to raise issues with you as and when they occur. As with disciplinary issues, an informal approach can defuse the situation and resolve problems before they get out of hand.

As an employer you need to ensure that your staff handbook, employees' contract of employment or company intranet sets out the procedure for raising grievances.

There are four steps to a formal grievance procedure.

1. The employee writes a letter to you, the employer, setting out the details of their complaint.

2. A meeting is held with both parties to establish the facts and try to agree a resolution. The employee has a legal right to bring a companion to the meeting with them.

3. After the meeting, you should write to the employee with your decision and what action, if any, you will take to resolve the grievance.

4. The employee has the right to appeal against your decision regarding the grievance.

Discipline and Grievances at Work: The Acas guide sets out best practice guidelines.

Equality and diversity

It is not only a legal requirement to treat employees fairly and considerately; it also makes good business sense. As your business grows, recruiting people from diverse backgrounds can help you build a powerful mix of skills and expertise and get new perspectives on what you do and how you do it. A diverse workforce can also give you the flexibility you may need to meet customer demands, and may even open up new markets you have never previously thought of.

Acas advises that it is unlawful to discriminate against people at work on the grounds of:

-✈ age

-✈ disability

-✈ gender reassignment

-✈ marriage and civil partnership

-✈ pregnancy and maternity

-✈ race

-✈ religion or belief

-✈ sex

-✈ sexual orientation.

Putting together an equality and diversity policy will demonstrate your commitment to these principles and send an important message to employees about how you plan to treat them – and how you expect them to behave towards each other.

You may find the following sample policy from Acas a helpful starting point. You can amend or add to it, depending on what is appropriate for your business. See also the EHRC's "Guidance for Employers" leaflet (www.equalityhumanrights.com/advice-and-guidance).

Acas's sample equality policy

[Company name] is committed to eliminating discrimination and encouraging diversity amongst our workforce. Our aim is that our workforce will be truly representative of all sections of society and each employee feels respected and able to give of their best.

To that end the purpose of this policy is to provide equality and fairness for all in our employment and not to discriminate on grounds of gender, marital status, race, ethnic origin, colour, nationality, national origin, disability, sexual orientation, religion or age. We oppose all forms of unlawful and unfair discrimination.

All employees, whether part-time, full-time or temporary, will be treated fairly and with respect. Selection for employment, promotion, training or any other benefit will be on the basis of aptitude and ability. All employees will be helped and encouraged to develop their full potential and the talents and resources of the workforce will be fully utilised to maximise the efficiency of the organisation.

Our commitment:

- To create an environment in which individual differences and the contributions of all our staff are recognised and valued.
- Every employee is entitled to a working environment that promotes dignity and respect to all. No form of intimidation, bullying or harassment will be tolerated.
- Training, development and progression opportunities are available to all staff.
- Equality in the workplace is good management practice and makes sound business sense.
- We will review all our employment practices and procedures to ensure fairness.
- Breaches of our equality policy will be regarded as misconduct and could lead to disciplinary proceedings.
- This policy is fully supported by senior management and has been agreed with trade unions and/or employee representatives. [Insert details if appropriate.]
- The policy will be monitored and reviewed annually.

Absence policy

Absenteeism can be a big problem for a small business. The impact of one person not pitching up to work when there are only a few of you keeping the wheels turning in the first place can be huge. Customers and clients get let down, phones go unanswered, orders don't go out and everyone else has to work doubly hard.

Of course, people – yourself included – are going to fall ill sometimes. A recent CIPD survey suggested that on average, people have 9.1 working days off sick per year. Colds and flu are the most common reason for absence, with 95% of employees citing this as the cause of their non-appearance at work. Stress also ranks highly, accounting for 13.4 million sick days per year. Third on the list come back pain, musculoskeletal injuries and recurring medical conditions.

As an employer, it can sometimes be hard to tell whether someone is genuinely ill or "throwing a sickie" because they've had a few too many the night before or fancy a day under the duvet. It can be difficult to find an appropriate balance between being concerned about your employee and wanting them back at work as soon as possible because you are worried about the impact on the business. On the one hand, you want to phone them up, find out how they are and see if there is anything you can do to help. On the other hand, you do need some idea of when they might be ready to return to work, so that you can make appropriate arrangements to cover their work if necessary.

Statement of "fitness for work"

There is a system in place which can help you manage these difficult conversations. If an employee is off short-term (up to seven days) you should ask them to fill in a "self-certificate" when they return, explaining the reasons for their absence. You can download a standard form (SC2) from the HMRC website (www.hmrc.gov.uk/forms/sc2.pdf).

Frequent short-term absences can be very disruptive. If you are faced with an employee who is often off work for a day here and there, you might want to sit down and have a chat to see if there is an underlying problem. Often an issue like unreliable child care, the need to care for a relative or work-related stress can be behind frequent periods off work.

Since April 2010, if someone has been off work for over seven days they are required to get a medical statement from their GP. On this document, which is known as a Statement of Fitness for Work, the GP can state that an individual is "fit", "unfit" or "may be fit" for work.

If this latter statement is given, it opens the door for you to have a conversation with your employee about whether you could organise a phased return to work or make some changes to their role which would help them get up and running more easily. Someone who has had an operation, for example, may find it easier to phase their return to work, coming in for half-days or two or three days a week to start with. These are issues you can discuss with your employee, and their GP can also provide guidance on what kind of work may or may not be appropriate.

For more information on the Statement of Fitness for Work you can read the Department for Work and Pensions guide for employers (www.dwp.gov.uk/fitnote).

Time off

There are also occasions when people will need to take time off to care for a sick relative or on "compassionate" grounds, such as a bereavement. An employee may want to request time off to go on a training course which is not directly related to their role, or to attend a medical appointment.

Equally, you may come across a situation where someone is called for jury service, is absent from work through circumstances outside their control such as adverse weather, or because they have been stranded abroad due to yet another "ash cloud".

It's a good idea to be clear about how you will manage these situations. Will the days absent be regarded as part of their annual leave? Will they be paid? In which situations do you feel it is acceptable to grant the time off?

Putting a policy together

A carefully thought-out policy on absence has benefits for both you and your employee.

It provides you with a clearly laid out procedure for managing absence proactively and consistently, and makes it clear to employees exactly what they need to do if they are off sick or need to take time off for any other reason.

The following sample absence policy from Acas will give you a "starter for 10", which you can adapt to suit the needs of your own business.

Acas's sample absence policy

We are committed to improving the health, wellbeing and attendance of all employees. We value the contribution our employees make to our success. So, when any employee is unable to be at work for any reason, we miss that contribution.

This absence policy explains:

- what we expect from managers and employees when handling absence
- how we will work to reduce levels of absence to no more than xx days per employee per year.

This policy has been written after consultation with employee representatives. We welcome the continued involvement of employees in implementing this policy.

Key principles
Our absence policy is based on the following principles.

1. As a responsible employer we undertake to provide payments to employees who are unable to attend work due to sickness (see the company sick pay scheme).
2. Regular, punctual attendance is an implied term of every employee's contract of employment – we ask each employee to take responsibility for achieving and maintaining good attendance.
3. We will support employees who have genuine grounds for absence for whatever reason. This support includes:
   a. special leave for necessary absences not caused by sickness
   b. a flexible approach to the taking of annual leave
   c. access to counsellors where necessary
   d. rehabilitation programme in cases of long-term sickness absence.
4. We will consider any advice given by the employee's GP on the "Statement of Fitness for Work". If the GP advises that an employee

"may be fit for work" we will discuss with the employee how we can help them get back to work – for example on flexible hours, or altered duties.

5. We will use an occupational health adviser, where appropriate, to
   a. Help identify the nature of the employee's illness.
   b. Advise the employee and their manager on the best way to improve the employee's health and wellbeing.

6. The company's disciplinary procedures will be used if an explanation for absence is not forthcoming or is not thought to be satisfactory.

7. We respect the confidentiality of all information relating to an employee's sickness. This policy will be implemented in line with all data protection legislation and the Access to Medical Records Act 1988.

Notification of absence

If an employee is going to be absent from work they should speak to their manager or deputy within an hour of their normal start time. They should also give:

- a clear indication of the nature of the illness
- a likely return date.

The manager will check with employees if there is any information they need about their current work. If the employee does not contact their manager by the required time the manager will attempt to contact the employee at home.

An employee may not always feel able to discuss their medical problems with their line manager. Managers will be sensitive to individual concerns and make alternative arrangements, where appropriate. For example, an employee may prefer to discuss health problems with a person of the same sex.

Evidence of incapacity

Employees can use the company self-certification arrangements for the first seven days' absence. Thereafter a "Statement of Fitness for Work" is required to cover every subsequent day.

If absence is likely to be protracted, ie more than four weeks continuously, there is a shared responsibility for the company and the employee to main contact at agreed intervals.

"May be Fit for some Work"

If the GP advises on the Statement of Fitness for Work that an employee "may be fit for work" we will discuss with the employee ways of helping them get back to work. This might mean talking about a phased return to work or amended duties.

If it is not possible to provide the support an employee needs to return to work – for example, by making the necessary workplace adjustments – or an employee feels unable to return then the Statement will be used in the same way as if the GP advised that the employee was "not fit for work".

Return to work discussions

Managers will discuss absences with employees when they return to work to establish:

- the reason for, and cause of, absence
- anything the manager or the company can do to help
- that the employee is fit to return to work.

If an employee's GP has advised that they "may be fit for work" the return to work discussion can also be used to agree in detail how their return to work might work best in practice.

A more formal review will be triggered by:

- frequent short-term absences
- long-term absence.

This review will look at any further action required to improve the employee's attendance and wellbeing. These trigger points are set by line managers and are available from personnel.

Absence due to disability/maternity
Absences relating to the disability of an employee or to pregnancy will be kept separate from sickness absence records. We refer employees to our Equality Policy – covering family policies and disability discrimination policies.

ACAS (www.acas.org.uk)

Other policies to consider

Use of company facilities

You may want to consider having a clear policy on appropriate use of company facilities such as the internet, email and telephone. It can sometimes be difficult to strike the right balance. On the one hand, the odd personal phone call doesn't do much harm. On the other, you don't want your employees to be spending time organising their social life on Facebook or picking up bargains on eBay when they are supposed to be working.

You do also need to bear in mind that inappropriate use of the internet could breach the security of your company's IT system or in extreme cases lead to legal action being taken against you. A chain email could introduce a virus into your system, or an employee may inadvertently word an email in a way which enters you into a binding contract with a client. Inappropriate use of language in an email could also lead to an accusation of harassment.

The lines between personal and business use can often be blurred. Your business, for example, might have a presence on Facebook and it could be beneficial if your employees are active on the site. You might well want to encourage an employee to spend time building their personal profile on LinkedIn, because it's a good way of promoting the expertise that exists in your company.

There always has to be a degree of trust involved about what is and isn't appropriate. Companies vary widely in their approach to this, so bear in mind that someone joining you from another business may be used to having unrestricted use of the internet and email.

The best way to avoid problems is to set boundaries up front by having a policy that makes it clear what is and isn't acceptable. Bear in mind that a policy shouldn't just be about what people are not allowed to do – it should also be about what is best practice.

Accepting that you can't stop people using social media (it's available at the touch of a button on their smartphones, after all) and involving employees in creating your policy is a good way to get their acceptance and buy-in. You might want to use the policy to promote the use of disclaimers at the end of emails, for example, or to make people aware of any password or security measures you have in place.

You would be wise to explain your internet and email policy to a new recruit during the induction process to avoid any misunderstandings later on, and you might even ask them to sign to say that they have read and understood it.

Check out the Gov.UK website for information on your employees' rights and responsibilities when they are using the internet or email in the course of their day-to-day work (www.gov.uk/monitoring-work-workers-rights).

Intellectual property

Whatever your business, it's likely that you will have some form of intellectual property. Intellectual property doesn't just relate to ground-breaking inventions; it also covers brands and logos, software, training materials, designs and creative work such as books, music and photography. If it's relevant to your business, you will no doubt have thought about protecting your intellectual property through patents and copyright. You do, however, also need to think about your intellectual property in relation to your employees.

If an employee is creating work that carries intellectual property rights on your behalf, the intellectual property generally belongs to you. In the case of any dispute, showing that a member of staff has an employment contract would usually be enough to prove that the intellectual property belongs to you. If this is likely to be a particularly important area for your business, however, you could consider adding a clause covering issues such as ownership and confidentiality to their contract.

The advice from Business Link is that it's also good practice to get employees to record in a logbook information about any innovative work they do.

A simple policy can also help to set boundaries and make sure there is no scope for misunderstanding about what belongs to who at a later date. Your policy should make it clear that any product or material developed by an employee while they're working for you is the property of the business, and that they are duty bound to keep information confidential.

Gov.UK has information on the best way to safeguard your intellectual property (www.gov.uk/intellectual-property-an-overview).

Drugs and alcohol

The statistics on drug and alcohol misuse in the UK are alarming. Research suggests that more than a quarter of men drink more than the recommended 21 units of alcohol a week and that 17% of women exceed the recommended 14 units per week. Thirty-six per cent of 16–59-year-olds have used one or more illicit drugs in their lifetime, with 12% having used an illicit drug at least once in the past year.

Drug and alcohol abuse undoubtedly has an effect on people's ability to attend work regularly and perform well, but the implications are wider-reaching. Someone who tips up to work while still under the influence is likely to be more at risk of having an accident or of endangering the safety of colleagues, customers or clients. Of course, it will also do your reputation no good at all if an employee is representing your business while hungover from the night before or – worse – evidently high on some kind of illegal substance.

As your business grows, you may well want to consider having a policy on drug and alcohol use at work – both to protect your interests and to make sure that employees have a clear understanding of what is and isn't acceptable. It's an issue you need to think about quite carefully. You need to give thought to what "the rules" are actually going to be and what will happen if people flout them. You also need to consider what stance you would take if it becomes apparent that an employee has a serious problem.

The CIPD's advice is:

> When dealing with alcohol or drug misuse at work, employers have to strike a balance between using the disciplinary procedure for conduct-related incidents and providing support where individuals have acknowledged they have a problem.

Startups Tip

Make sure any rules you do set are not at odds with the "culture" that exists in your business. It's no good having a zero tolerance policy on alcohol if it's common practice for your team to head off to the pub every lunchtime.

Setting the rules

You are perfectly entitled to ban drinking during working hours if you feel that is appropriate. For some businesses, this is critical – for example, if your staff are working on construction sites or using dangerous equipment, or if driving takes up a significant part of their day. In this case, you will want to make the "rules" very strict and you will need to be very specific about what is and isn't acceptable.

In other environments, you may feel that the odd drink to celebrate a big business win, for example, is absolutely fine, or that you don't mind people occasionally going to the pub at lunchtime provided they don't come back the worse for wear and incapable of doing their job for the rest of the afternoon.

In general, any policy you put together should:

→ make the rules about alcohol and drug use in the workplace crystal clear

→ set out the procedure that will be used to deal with any problems that do occur

→ link with existing policies on disciplinary procedure and absence at work

→ make it clear to employees that the business will support them if they have a serious dependency and need to seek help.

You might also want to consider whether your policy should apply to any temporary staff or contractors who are carrying out work on your behalf.

In its guide on *Managing Drug and Alcohol Misuse at Work*, the CIPD sets out some example statements that you might want to include in a drugs and alcohol policy.

Options include the following.

→ Employees are responsible for maintaining sensible and safe drinking levels.

→ Employees are not allowed to drink during working hours. This includes meal breaks and on call duties.

→ No employee is banned from drinking, but they must maintain professional conduct during working hours.

→ No employee should report to duty within certain hours of drinking alcohol.

→ No employee may possess, consume or provide drugs or alcohol while on duty (except prescription drugs prescribed to the individual).

→ No employee shall report for work while under the influence of drugs.

→ Employees on prescribed medication that may affect their ability to perform their duties must notify the company before reporting for duty.

There's no right or wrong answer. It's a case of choosing the statements that best meet the needs of your business and striking a balance between being restrictive and being responsible.

Check out the CIPD's sample policy, which may provide a useful template against which to draft your own policy (www.cipd.co.uk, you may need to become a member to access this).

Checklist

☑ Make sure you have a system in place to keep up to date with changes in employment law (an HR consultant or employment lawyer will be able to help you).

☑ Draw up a health and safety policy that reflects the risks in your particular business.

☑ Put together a disciplinary procedure that makes it clear what behaviour is acceptable and what process will be used if problems arise.

☑ Make sure you are familiar with the key stages of the formal grievance procedure, so you know exactly what to do if it is invoked by one of your employees.

☑ Develop an equality and diversity policy to demonstrate to your employees that you take the issue seriously – and that you expect them to do the same.

☑ Take time out to think about how you will manage employee absence – both planned and unplanned – in your business.

☑ Consider which non-mandatory policies may be relevant for your business. Internet and email use, drug and alcohol use and intellectual property are among those you might like to consider.

↩ CHAPTER 10
Key employment legislation

📖 **What's in this chapter?**

The thought of having to deal with masses of
complicated employment legislation can be daunting
for the owner of a fledgling business, but don't despair,
help is at hand!

In this chapter we'll cover:

→ how much maternity and paternity leave your
employees are entitled to

→ the ins and outs of maternity pay

→ how to manage return to work after
maternity

→ your obligations with regard to adoption leave

→ what you need to know about flexible working
legislation — and why it can be a positive
boon for your business

→ recent changes to the laws on retirement and how this will affect your business

→ changes to rules on Workplace pensions: what you are obliged to do and when you have to do it.

You'll no doubt be pleased to hear that the coalition government has recognised that small businesses are struggling to cope with too much bureaucracy and red tape, and has taken action to improve the situation. It has pledged, for example, that businesses with fewer than 10 staff will be exempt from new employment regulations for three years. This is good news for the 4.6 million "micro-firms" who will be spared the immediate need to spend hours getting their heads round complicated rules and filling in forms.

There are, however, some key pieces of existing legislation that do apply – and that you need to be aware of as soon as you start to take people on. In particular, you need to be familiar with the legislation on:

-> maternity, paternity and adoption

-> flexible working

-> retirement

-> pensions.

Maternity, paternity and adoption

We have come a long way from the days when women were expected to retire from work after their marriages, and later decades when pregnant women were treated almost like unexploded bombs in the workplace and ushered out of the door marked "exit" well before they got TOO BIG.

In 2011, the right of dads to share the care in the first year of their child's life was enshrined in the statute books. What impact this will have and how it will affect business, only time will tell, but employers need to be aware that it is not just female employees who may be planning to go on leave when there's a new arrival in the family.

Maternity leave

Every expectant mother working in the UK is entitled to take up to 52 weeks' statutory maternity leave (SML) commencing around the time her baby is born. Her contract of employment continues throughout the period of her leave, though she is not expected to come in to work, except for keeping in touch (KIT) days (see below). She must inform you, preferably in writing, by the 15th week before the baby is due that she is expecting a baby, the date the baby is due and the date she wants her maternity leave to start. However, it is better if she tells you earlier as you have a legal duty to protect her health and safety during pregnancy

Maternity leave can begin at any time from the 11th week before the baby is due. If the employee is off work for any reason relating to the pregnancy from the fourth week before the baby is due, maternity leave will automatically start from that date.

Ask your employee for medical certificate MATB1, usually issued to the expectant mum by her midwife or GP.

Pregnant women have certain statutory rights, including:

→ the right to take paid time off work for antenatal care (once she has told you she is expecting)

→ the right to work in a safe environment

→ the right to claim discrimination and unfair dismissal if dismissed because of pregnancy or maternity leave

→ the right to take up to 52 weeks' maternity leave

→ the right (for some women) to statutory maternity pay (SMP)

→ the right to return to work after she has had her baby. A refusal to allow her to return to work will be viewed as dismissal and will also be discrimination.

You must review the work she does and any risks involved in the job, and make any changes necessary to protect the health of the employee and their unborn child. Risks can include lifting or carrying heavy loads, standing or sitting for long periods, exposure to toxic substances and long working hours. If it is not possible to make the necessary changes and no other suitable work is available, the individual should be suspended from work on full pay.

The absolute minimum time new mums must take off after the birth is two weeks – four if she works in a factory – and it is your responsibility as an employer to ensure that she doesn't return to work any earlier. In 2009, the French justice minister Rachida Dati caused something of a furore when she returned to work just five days after giving birth. Three weeks later she "resigned" amid rumours that she had been under pressure to get back behind the ministerial desk so soon after her baby daughter was born.

If things go wrong

Everyone hopes for a happy outcome to a pregnancy, but if an employee gives birth to a stillborn baby after the 24th week of pregnancy she is still entitled to maternity leave. If the baby is born alive, either full term or prematurely, but later dies, the mother is still entitled to maternity leave. If she has the misfortune to miscarry before the end of the 24th week of pregnancy she is not entitled to maternity leave.

As a responsible employer you could offer sick leave or compassionate leave to give them time to recover from the emotional and physical impact of the miscarriage. Sick leave following miscarriage, or sick leave for a pregnancy-related illness, should be recorded separately from any other kinds of illness on an individual's sickness absence records. The woman may be entitled to sick pay if you include this in your contract of employment or, alternatively, to statutory sick pay.

Maternity pay

During the first 26 weeks – called ordinary maternity leave (OML) – employees are entitled to the same rights under their contract of employment as if she were still at work, including building up holiday entitlement and receiving any pay increases. During this period, normal pay is replaced by SMP – unless enhanced pay benefits are included in their contract of employment or she doesn't qualify for this pay, in which case she may qualify for maternity allowance (MA).

SMP is recoverable, should be paid in the usual way as salary (ie weekly or monthly) and as it counts as earnings, tax and NICs should be deducted. It is paid for up to 39 weeks, starting from the 11th week before the baby is due at the earliest, or the week following the week the baby is born at the latest. For the first six weeks of maternity leave

SMP is paid at 90% of the employee's average gross weekly earnings. For the remaining 33 weeks it is paid either at 90% of average gross weekly earnings or, currently, £135.45 per week, whichever is the lower figure. To qualify for SMP, the employee must have worked for you for at least 26 weeks up to the 15th week before the week the baby is due.

According to the latest information from HMRC, if your total NICs payments are £45,000 a year or less, you will be able to recover 103% of the SMP that you pay. This is to compensate you for the employer's NICs you have to pay on top of the SMP.

If your total National Insurance payments are more than £45,000 a year, you can recover 92% of the SMP you have to pay. You can recover the payments by deducting them from your monthly PAYE payments. You will need to keep the following information for your records:

-⏵ form MATB1 (mentioned above)

-⏵ the payment dates and amount paid using HMRC form SMP2

-⏵ the date the pay period began

-⏵ any weeks in the 39-week period when SMP was not paid and the reason for this.

You must also keep records of amounts paid and recovered on your employee payroll records and in the year end summary forms you submit to HMRC. Quick answers to common questions on SMP can be found on the HMRC website (www.hmrc.gov.uk).

Enhanced benefits

Some employers offer enhanced maternity leave and pay benefits on a contractual or discretionary basis. For example, Deutsche Bank in the UK gives four months of paid maternity/paternity leave following the birth or adoption of a child to members of staff who are the infant's primary caregivers. The bank also has a company crèche as well as offering childcare vouchers as an option in its staff benefits package.

Keeping in touch

Under recent legislation, women on maternity leave can work up to 10 days during this period without affecting their right to maternity leave or pay. These are called keeping in touch (KIT) days. Any amount of work done on a KIT day counts as one day: if your employee comes in for a team meeting or a conference with an important client and the meeting only takes an hour or two, she will have used up one of her KIT days.

Many employers view KIT days as a useful way of keeping the employee in the organisational loop and making her return to work that much easier. They are optional for both parties – you cannot insist that your employee works a KIT day and neither can she insist on doing KIT days if it doesn't suit you.

Agree with your employee before she goes on leave how much you will pay her for any KIT days worked, in addition to SMP entitlement.

Returning to work

Your employee will be due to return to work when her 52 weeks' maternity leave comes to an end. If she wants to return earlier, she must give you at least eight weeks' notice. If she decides not to return to work, she should give you notice in the normal way under the terms of her contract of employment.

If she returns to work after 26 weeks – the period called ordinary maternity leave (OML) – she is entitled to return to her original job under the same terms and conditions as if she had not been away. If she returns during the second 26-week period of maternity leave – called additional maternity leave (AML) – she is entitled to the same terms and conditions as she enjoyed previously, but not to the same job – if you can show that this is not possible because, for example, the role no longer exists. If a week is a long time in politics, a year is a very long time in the life of a business, particularly a small business. Reshuffles, recessions or restructuring mean that roles can and do change. However, you must offer the returnee an alternative position with the same terms and conditions as she had before.

Flexible working

An employee returning to work following the birth of a child is entitled to request to work flexibly, for example working fewer hours and/or working from home. Requests must be made in writing, should be considered seriously and can only be refused if there is a clear business case for doing so. If this situation should arise, arrange a meeting and try to find a solution that suits both the business and the parent.

Adoption

No matter how many hours an employee works or how much they are paid, they are entitled to statutory adoption leave of 52 weeks provided they have worked continuously for you for at least 26 weeks before the beginning of the week when they are matched to a child by an adoption agency.

Leave can start on the day the child starts living with the adoptive parent or up to 14 days before it is due to live with its new family. KIT days can be taken by adoptive parents – see above.

To qualify for statutory adoption pay of up to 39 weeks, paid at the same rate as maternity pay, your employee must meet the qualifying criteria for adoption leave and should also produce documentary proof, usually a "matching certificate" from the adoption agency. The agency must be recognised in the UK.

Private adoptions, adopting stepchildren, becoming a special guardian or having a child through surrogacy does not qualify the individual for statutory leave or pay. If such a situation occurs, you might consider allowing the individual to take a period of paid or unpaid holiday or leave.

Dads and adoptive dads

New rules introduced recently give dads the opportunity to share the baby's care for up to 26 weeks. This new entitlement is called additional paternity leave and is in addition to the one- or two-week ordinary paternity leave (OPL) new dads are entitled to. The weeks of ordinary leave have to run consecutively – not on separate days – and must be taken within eight weeks of the baby's birth or adoption of the child.

To qualify for OPL, your employee must have worked for you for at least 26 weeks by either the end of the 15th week before the start of the week when the baby is due or, for adoptive fathers, the end of the week he is notified that they have been matched with a child.

For those qualifying for and taking this leave, the current weekly rate of ordinary statutory paternity pay (OSPP) is £135.45 or 90% of the employee's average weekly salary, whichever is lower. You will be able to recover 100% of this payment plus 3% to compensate you for the employer's NICs you have to pay on it (from April 2011) through PAYE.

Dads wishing to take over full-time care of their baby have to meet the same qualifying conditions as for OPL (above). In addition, the mother of the child must have returned to work and ceased claiming any relevant payments.

Dads who qualify for and take extended leave to look after their child may be entitled to additional statutory paternity pay (ASPP), depending on how long they have worked for you, how much they earn and when the baby is due or adopted. You should be able to recover most or all of these payments in the same way as maternity pay is recovered, through the PAYE system.

Parental leave

As an employer, you also need to be aware that employees with young or disabled children are entitled to apply for unpaid parental leave. Employees are entitled to a maximum of four weeks' parental leave in any one year per each individual child, although you can agree to grant more if you wish.

They can only take this parental leave either before the child's fifth birthday, before the fifth anniversary of an adopted child's placement with them (or their 18th birthday if this is earlier) or, in the case of a disabled child, before their 18th birthday. They need to give you 21 days' notice of the proposed start and end dates of the leave and must take it in multiples of one week. The exception to this is if their child is disabled, in which case the leave can be taken as individual days.

In a difficult economic climate, it's unlikely that you will receive many applications for parental leave – not many employees can afford to take unpaid time off work. Some employees do, however, use parental leave as a way of delaying their return to work after maternity leave (which they are entitled to do provided they have given you the necessary notice).

Employees may also request parental leave in order to be with a child who is going into hospital, for example, or to settle a toddler down into a new nursery. In other words, the reason for the leave needs to be to take care of a child, and the circumstances need to be pre-planned. Parental leave is not suitable for times when a child suddenly falls ill or childcare arrangements break down, as this would make it impossible to give the necessary period of notice.

In an unforeseen situation, employees have the right to a reasonable amount of unpaid time off to allow them to deal with an emergency involving a child – or indeed any other dependent. There is no fixed time for this kind of leave – the rule of thumb is that it should be sufficient time for them to deal with the immediate problem and put plans in place for going forward.

Formulating policy

Don't wait until the stork hovers over your workplace. Formulate a policy on staff taking maternity, paternity and adoption leave, and include the details in your standard contract of employment and/or staff handbook. Keep up to date with changing legislation by checking the HMRC website regularly.

Other useful sources of information about maternity, paternity and adoption leave and pay include Citizens Advice and Acas (helpline 08457 474747).

> You must provide working mums who are breastfeeding their babies with a place to rest and suitable rest periods, bearing in mind that the loos are not suitable for this purpose.

Baby talk

- SMP – statutory maternity pay (up to 39 weeks)
- MA – maternity allowance (for those not eligible for SMP)
- SML – statutory maternity leave (up to 52 weeks)
- OML – ordinary maternity leave (first 26 weeks)
- AML – additional maternity leave (following 26 weeks)
- MATB1 – medical certificate issued by GP or midwife to expectant mum
- KIT – keeping in touch days (up to 10 days without losing SML or SMP)
- SAL – statutory adoption leave (up to 52 weeks)
- SAP – statutory adoption pay (up to 39 weeks)
- OPL – ordinary paternity leave (one or two weeks taken consecutively)
- OSPP – ordinary statutory paternity pay (one or two weeks)
- APL – additional paternity leave (up to 26 weeks)
- ASPP – additional statutory paternity pay (up to 26 weeks)

Flexible working

The days when everyone worked 9 to 5, Monday to Friday are long gone. You only have to look around at your friends and family to see the number of flexible working arrangements that are now common practice in businesses of all types and sizes.

Flexible working isn't just a convenience for your employees, it's a way of working that can bring real bottom-line benefits to your business – even if you only have one or two staff. In certain circumstances, you also have a legal requirement to seriously consider flexible working requests from existing employees.

As an employer, depending on the nature of your business, flexible working can help you:

→ attract a wider, more diverse pool of candidates for vacancies, for example highly skilled women who do not want to work full-time because of family commitments but who can still make a valuable contribution to your business

→ extend the number of hours your business is able to respond to customers. A shop, for example, might be able to close later or open seven days a week if it has a pool of people working flexible, part-time hours. If you have a lot of telephone contact with customers, you might be able to extend the amount of time you are available to respond to enquiries

-▷ improve your competitiveness by being more fleet of foot when it comes to responding to changes in customer demands

-▷ keep hold of valuable employees whose circumstances may have changed since they first joined you

-▷ be more cost-effective and efficient. You can save on overheads, for example, if you allow people to work from home; or you can keep the wheels of production machinery turning 24/7 by offering flexible shifts

-▷ build a team of committed, loyal employees who are prepared to give you their best because you have understood and responded to their need to achieve better work–life balance.

For your employees, the opportunity to work flexibly often means they can:

-▷ achieve a better work–life balance

-▷ reduce stress levels

-▷ take control of their workload and manage it more effectively

-▷ avoid wasting valuable time commuting at peak times.

Types of flexible working

Mention the term "flexible working" and people have a tendency to immediately think of either part-time working or job sharing. In fact, there are numerous ways you can offer flexible working arrangements – it's just a case of finding an option that meets the needs of your business and works well for your employees.

The main types of flexible working are listed below.

Part-time

This is where your employees work less than standard full-time hours, for example three days per week or every day 10am–2pm. It's important to remember that part-time workers have the same employment rights as full-time employees. They are entitled to receive the same rates of pay, for example, and to annual leave on a pro rata basis.

Job share

This is when two employees share one job, splitting the days/hours between them as appropriate. This might mean one employee working the morning while the other does the afternoon; or they may split the week between them, with a handover period in the middle. Managed properly, it can be an extremely effective arrangement which gives you lots of flexibility and means the job is always covered.

Flexi-time

Flexi-time is a great way to help employees avoid peak travelling times or fit domestic responsibilities around their work commitments. Usually, it means that your staff are contracted to work a set number of hours per week, but they can choose when they do those hours within certain core times. So someone might chose to work 8am–4pm, for example, so they can avoid the rush hour, or to start at 9.30am so they can do the school run on their way to work.

Compressed working hours

Employees work a set number of hours, but fit the time into fewer working days, for example working four days instead of five. This can work particularly well if you have a business that operates outside the standard 9 to 5 working day and you need people to cover longer opening hours.

Term-time working

This is a great way to attract and retain female employees who are trying to juggle work and family demands. Staff are employed on a permanent contract, but take either paid or unpaid leave during the school holidays. This wouldn't work for every business, but is worth considering if you can arrange projects around these key times or are able to bring in temporary cover during the holidays.

Home working

Home working is an option that is well worth considering if the type of business you are running doesn't need people to be physically present in your office all the time. It means that you can save significantly on office overheads and can attract candidates from a wider geographical area.

Employers usually supply home workers with a computer, printer, mobile phone and whatever other equipment is required. Don't forget that health and safety rules apply to home workers too – so it's important to check that their work station is appropriate and that any equipment is safe.

Managing home workers sometimes calls for a shift in mindset and an emphasis on tasks completed rather than hours worked. It's also important to put proper communication mechanisms in place, so that your home-workers are fully involved and part of the team.

Right to request flexible working

Of course, any prospective (or existing) employee can ask to work outside the standard 9 to 5 and, given some of the advantages, it's definitely worth discussing the options with them.

Some staff, however, have a statutory right to request flexible working, and as an employer you are obliged to seriously consider their request. This statutory right applies to parents of children under the age of 17 (or 18 if the child is disabled) or those who are carers. In order to be eligible the individual must have worked for you continuously for more than 26 weeks and cannot already have used the legislation to make an application during the previous 12 months.

It's worth keeping an eye out for possible changes to this legislation in the months ahead. There are plans to extend the right to request flexible working to those with children under 18 and eventually to all employees, but these are still under discussion.

If an employee makes a request to work flexibly, you cannot simply say no. You need to show that there are valid business reasons for your refusal. You might feel, for example, that it would affect your ability to meet customer demands or that the quality of service you are able to offer would decline.

You don't have to automatically say yes either. In many cases, requests for flexible working can quite easily be accommodated and may well be advantageous to your business – but you need to make sure that the changes your employee is requesting are feasible and will not have a detrimental impact on your operation.

There is a set procedure that has to be followed if one of your employees exercises their statutory right to request flexible working.

-> You are obliged to arrange a meeting with them within 28 days to discuss the application.

-> You have 14 days to make a decision about whether to accept the proposal.

-> If you refuse, you will need to show that there are valid business reasons for turning the application down.

-> If the employee is not happy with your decision, they can appeal, and you have 14 days in which to arrange an appeal meeting.

-> You have 14 days in which to make a decision based on the discussions you have had at this internal appeal meeting.

-> If you still decide to turn down the application, the employee then has a further right to appeal, either by invoking your company's formal grievance procedure, by using the Acas arbitration scheme or by taking their case to an employment tribunal.

These are the basic steps of the procedure. You can find the full detail of the legislation and an advice leaflet on the ACAS website (www.acas.org.uk). The CIPD also publishes a useful fact sheet on flexible working www.cipd.co.uk/hr-resources/factsheets/flexible-working.aspx.

Retirement

If you already employ or are planning to take on older workers, it's important to be aware of the legislation on retirement.

Recent changes to the law mean that there is no longer a set age at which people have to retire. The previous default retirement age (DRA) of 65 was abolished in early 2011 and from now on, employees can retire when they are ready to. If you, as an employer, want someone to retire, you can no longer force them to do so unless it can be "objectively justified". This means that you need to think carefully about how you approach the whole issue of retirement with an employee, to make sure you are not inadvertently leaving yourself open to claims of unfair dismissal or discrimination.

This shouldn't deter you from employing older workers. They can be reliable, committed employees with a wealth of knowledge and experience to bring to your business. It's a misconception that older people are likely to be ill more often. Research shows that in general they are reliable, committed employees who actually take less sick leave than their younger colleagues. Thanks to advances in medicine, people are now living longer and are physically able to work for longer than in the past – plus, of course, many want to continue working for financial reasons or simply because they enjoy it.

The key to successfully managing retirement without falling foul of the law is to have regular, open and honest discussions with your employees. If the lines of communication are open, it makes it much easier for people to talk about their future plans and to raise any ideas or concerns they may have. It's good practice to have these kinds of discussions with all employees, not just older workers, at least on an annual basis. You can do this as part of a regular performance appraisal or as a separate, more informal discussion. It's a great opportunity to talk about how staff are performing against any targets you may have set them and what training they may need to help them develop further. You can talk about where you see the business going in the future, and ask people about their own aims and how they see themselves in the short, medium and longer term.

Acas advises that when you are having these discussions with older workers, it's a good idea to avoid direct questions like "Are you planning to retire in the near future?" A more appropriate approach would be to ask people about their future plans in general. This will give employees the opportunity to tell you what they have in mind and to talk about any changes they might want to make in the lead-up to their retirement. It's quite common, for example, for people to want to gradually reduce their working hours, or to perhaps move to a less pressurised role. Bear in mind that the run-up to retirement can be a great time to get older employees to act as mentors and coaches to less experience colleagues.

Once someone has told you they want to retire, you can start to talk to put plans in place and come to an agreement about a suitable date. It's important to recognise that people do have the right to change their mind about what they say in these discussions. You are only entitled to hold them to a retirement date if they have given you formal notice.

In the majority of cases, this approach should allow you and your employee to plan together for a successful retirement. The situation becomes more complicated, however, if an employee is not performing well in their role or if you feel there are legitimate grounds to ask them to retire at a set age.

It is still possible to retire an employee lawfully at a set age if you can show that this meets a legitimate aim. You may be concerned, for example, about the health and safety of employees or your customers. Bear in mind that if you decide to go down this route, it is not likely to be easy and you will have to provide evidence to show that your request can be objectively justified.

The other option open to you is to dismiss someone, following the usual procedures. Remember that for a dismissal to be deemed fair it has to be related to conduct, capability, redundancy, statutory ban or some other substantial reason (see the section on dismissal, p. 147)

You can find more detailed guidance about retiring employees, plus a guide to "Working Without the Default Retirement Age", on the Acas website (www.acas.org.uk). The CIPD also publishes a handy fact sheet on the default retirement age (www.cipd.co.uk/hr-resources/ factsheets/default-retirement-age.aspx).

Pensions

There are big changes afoot to the rules about workplace pensions which will affect all businesses over the next few years, regardless of their size and the number of people they employ. New legislation has been brought in to encourage people to save for their retirement, so they don't have to rely on the state pension. People in the UK today can expect to live longer than ever before, yet only 45% of the UK workforce currently has any kind of workplace pension.

From October 2012, employers are obliged to provide access to a workplace pension scheme for most workers. They have to automatically enrol employees either in their own pension scheme – if this meets the required standards – or in the new state-sponsored National Employment Savings Trust (NEST). Large firms will be the first to have to comply with the legislation, which will be gradually rolled out to smaller employers, with the aim that every business will be taking part by April 2017.

Firms with fewer than 30 qualifying workers are required to implement the scheme between 1 January 2016 and 1 April 2017, while companies that begin trading between April 2012 and September 2017 are required to meet implementation dates between 1 May 2017 and 1 February 2018. It may seem some way off, but it is worth being aware of the legislation so that you can plan ahead – and there is nothing to stop you getting involved before the final deadline.

The new legislation states that employers will need to:

→ automatically enrol and pay minimum contributions for any workers aged at least 22 but under 65, depending on when they were born, who earn more than £8,105 in a year. (This figure is subject to change between 2012 and 2017)

→ enrol and pay contributions for workers aged 16–75 who earn more than £5,564 and who ask to be enrolled.

The employer contribution will eventually be a minimum of 3% of earnings for staff who are opted in. The level of contribution will also be phased in, starting at 1% and rising to 3% by 2017. Employees who are auto-enrolled in schemes will have the opportunity to opt out if they want to, but they will have to do this within 90 days.

National Employment Savings Trust (NEST)

The NEST scheme will provide small businesses with a simple and convenient way to comply with the legislation. The idea is that it will also make it easy for individuals to build up a retirement "pot", which will stay with them if they stop working or change employers.

It's easy to register and get up and running with the system, and there is no ongoing admin. If someone leaves the business their pension follows them. Employees will have access to information about their pension online 24/7, with no need to go through their employer. Getting started will just involve filling in a simple online registration form with details of your business, how many people you employ and your PAYE and bank details. You can find out more from the NEST website (www.nestpensions.org.uk), which has a handy employer set-up guide which you can download for free. You can also contact NEST by telephone (030 0303 1947) or email (employerenquiries@ nestcorporation.org.uk).

Checklist

☑ Familiarise yourself with the legislation on maternity, paternity and adoption — and make sure you keep up to date with any changes.

☑ Consider seriously how you can use flexible working to benefit your business.

☑ Gen up on the recent changes to regulations affecting retirement so that you are prepared should the situation arise.

☑ Establish how you will deal with your obligation to provide access to a workplace pension for your employees.

☑ Consider using the services of an HR consultant or employment lawyer to help you keep up to date with ongoing changes to employment legislation.

☑ Remember that ignorance is not an excuse — you have a duty to be aware of employment law and to act accordingly.

↪ CHAPTER 11

Getting your employee off to a good start

📖 What's in this chapter?

What do you need to do to make sure your new recruit hits the ground running and starts to deliver results for your business straightaway? An effective induction programme, coupled with a system of regular appraisals and training, will go a long way to ensuring ongoing good performance.

This chapter will cover:

→ the key elements of a successful induction programme

→ how to use a probation period wisely

→ why appraisals are important – and how to do them well

→ why it's important to invest in training – and some ideas for how to do it cost-effectively.

f you've gone to the time and trouble of recruiting someone, it makes sense to ensure they get off to the best possible start in their new role. All too often, new recruits are thrown in at the deep end and expected to just get on with it without any help. They waste hours trying to work out how the computer system works or where to find answers to basic questions, simply because no one has taken the time and trouble to explain "how we do things around here".

A small investment of time up front can make all the difference – to the person's confidence, to their ability to get up to speed quickly with their role and to how comfortable they feel working for your business.

If people don't feel supported in their job, they will quickly become demoralised, will lose their enthusiasm for the job and certainly won't fulfil their potential. In the worst case scenario, they may even decide to leave – which means you will have to start the whole recruitment process all over again.

Induction

The key to getting your new employees to hit the ground running is to put together a simple but effective induction programme. Starting a new job is always stressful and people need help to settle in to their new surroundings and find their place in the team. A timely and well thought out induction can:

-↗ make people feel welcome

-↗ create clarity about their role and what they are expected to achieve

-↗ help them understand "the way we do things around here"

-↗ ensure they are productive from day one.

The nature and scope of an induction programme will vary according to the size and needs of your business. As a general rule, however, a good induction should include the following elements.

→ **Company background:** a brief introduction to the business, its products or services, and, if appropriate, its culture, values and brand.

→ **The role:** clarify the scope of the role and how it fits into the team and the wider business set-up.

→ **The key people:** an introduction to the key people the new recruit will come across. These might be other employees (if you have more than one), or key client or supplier contacts.

→ **Terms and conditions:** absence and holiday procedures, disciplinary and grievance policy, rewards and benefits, internet and email policies.

→ **Introduction to the premises:** location of the kitchen/toilets, post and photocopying facilities, plus details of any specific parking or security arrangements.

→ **Health and safety:** making people aware of your health and safety policy is a legal requirement. This should cover issues such as the evacuation procedure, first aid facilities, accident reporting system, need for protective clothing if appropriate.

Putting an induction together doesn't have to be a time-consuming task. Much of the information about policies, for example, may already be outlined in your staff handbook and people will only need a quick introduction.

It's not necessary to put together a formal presentation either – although this may be worthwhile if you have several new recruits starting at the same time.

Research has shown that taking the time to introduce people properly to the business definitely reaps rewards. They are more likely to be effective quickly in their new role and less likely to leave within the first few months, landing you with the cost and inconvenience of having to recruit again.

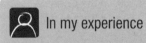
In my experience

Angela Fletcher, Rock Recruitment

Angela Fletcher started Rock Recruitment from an office in her loft four years ago. Today she has high street premises and a staff of nine, who manage recruitment for clients across a range of sectors.

Angela believes a thorough induction process is the key to making sure that employees are effective in their roles from an early stage – and that they stay the course. During their first week in the business, new recruits shadow one of their senior colleagues, spending time in different departments and getting familiar with systems and procedures. Angela sits down personally with them at the end of every day to answer any questions and make sure the induction is going according to plan.

Over the next three weeks, new employees accompany fellow consultants on client visits and gradually start to spend time on their own, building up their own network of contacts. This is backed up by a team meeting that is held every morning to discuss what's on everyone's agenda for the day.

"We start every day together as a team, discuss what we are working on and learn from each other," says Angela. Once the new recruit is up and running, they have a monthly one-to-one with their manager, as well as a more formal three-month review with Angela herself. "We try to be very supportive and it's important to keep the lines of communication open so that everyone knows what's expected," she says.

Probationary period

You may have decided to hire someone subject to a successful trial or probationary period. This can be a useful way of making sure the candidate has the skills you need and is definitely the right person for the job. It's also helpful if you have taken someone on with a view to training them in a particular skill.

The length of a probationary period will vary according to the job and how long it will take for the employee to pick up the necessary knowledge and competencies or show what they're made of. Three months is a common timeframe. You can extend the probationary period if you are broadly happy with the candidate and feel they just need a bit more time to get the skills for the job firmly under their belt.

Make sure you use the probationary period wisely. Don't just leave your new recruit to flounder without any support or guidance. The aim should be to set them up for success by providing any necessary training and coaching and mentoring them to perform well in their new role.

If, after all, your best efforts the employee doesn't come up to scratch, you can decide to withdraw the offer at the end of their probationary period. You need to give them whatever period of notice is set out in their written statement (see p. 48) and to explain clearly why you do not feel it is appropriate to keep them on.

You need to be aware that if you dismiss an employee either during or at the end of their probationary period, they may be able to claim breach of contract, for example if you haven't given them the training you had previously committed to providing.

Appraisals

Once you've got someone successfully up and running, it's important to plan how you will continue to manage their performance on an ongoing basis.

It's good practice to have regular appraisals with your team, so that you can review how the job is going, have an open discussion with people about what they're doing well and whether there are areas where they might need further training or support.

Managed well, appraisals are a great way of keeping employees motivated and developing their loyalty and commitment. If they can see you are interested in them and prepared to invest in their development, they are much more likely to go the extra mile. An appraisal (or development discussion, as they are sometimes called) is also a good opportunity to keep employees up to date with your plans for the business, so that they can see where they fit in and what opportunities might be open to them in the future. Handled badly, however, an appraisal can leave people feeling disengaged, resentful and under-valued. The key is to sandwich any constructive criticism you may have between compliments about what is going well, so that the individual doesn't feel they are being got at. Make sure you give employees a fair chance to respond to any negative feedback and show that you are willing to find ways to help them improve their performance or tackle any problem areas.

Natalie Sanderson, a director at Ascent PR, says:

> Appraisals are about putting time and thought into your team and their roles in the organisation – that's pretty important stuff. It's about giving feedback, recognising what employees are great at, how they can progress further, where their weaknesses lie, and of course, how these can be addressed. It's also an opportunity to talk. Talking with a person one-to-one helps you to make a connection and find out what makes them tick. The appraisal gives the employee an opportunity to be heard in an environment where they feel relaxed and able to share their thoughts.

There are no set rules about how often to hold an appraisal – you can decide what suits you best. Twice a year is probably a sensible timescale for most businesses, but whatever you decide, make sure you stick to your planned schedule and don't let the discussions slip.

Of course, this doesn't mean that you can't talk to staff about their performance between formal appraisals. Indeed, if there are problem areas it's best to raise these early, so that there are no nasty surprises for the employee when their appraisal comes around. You can't assume that they will be aware of any issues you may have with their work, so it's best to air any concerns as soon as possible. Try to do this in an informal, non-confrontational way, so that you can have an honest discussion about your expectations and what you can do to help your employee meet them.

The following checklist should help you plan for a positive and successful appraisal.

⇢ Notify employees that you plan to hold an appraisal well in advance: at least two weeks is advisable. This will give both you and the individual a chance to prepare properly for the discussion.

⇢ Find a room or space to hold the appraisal where you can talk privately and without being interrupted.

⇢ Remember that people are often nervous about appraisals, so do your best to make it a friendly, positive discussion and to put them at their ease.

⇢ Make sure you allow enough time for a proper discussion. It will give the wrong message if you are constantly checking your watch and clearly itching to move on to the next meeting.

⇢ Make sure you have thought in advance about the key areas you want to cover during the appraisal.

⇢ Seek feedback from others who work alongside your employee (or from clients they regularly deal with) so that you have a full picture of their performance and capabilities.

⇢ Use the opportunity to praise the individual for those aspects of the job they are doing really well – and discuss how you might make even better use of their talents and capabilities.

⇢ Highlight any areas where you feel the employee could benefit from further development and have an open discussion with them about the best ways to improve their performance in these particular tasks.

⇢ Remember that an appraisal is a two-way street. Give the individual plenty of opportunity to raise their own issues, ideas and ambitions for the future.

⇢ Ask open questions to encourage them to take an active role in the discussion. "Where do you feel you are contributing well?"

and "What can I do to support you better in achieving your targets/objectives?" are a couple of examples.

-▷ Agree on the actions that need to be taken as a result of your discussion.

-▷ Make sure any objectives you have set for your employee are SMART (specific, measurable, achievable, relevant and time-based).

-▷ Make sure you follow up on whatever is agreed.

Setting employees up for success

A final word about training: you might feel that as a small business, you don't have the budget to invest in developing your people – or indeed in developing yourself.

It's important to recognise, however, that in today's fast-moving, competitive environment, we all need to keep developing in order to stand still.

If you are serious about growing your business, you need to make sure you are helping your employees maximise their potential. That means investing some time and effort in developing their skills and talents, so that they can deliver an even better service to clients and customers and help you spot and develop new markets and opportunities.

Training doesn't have to be expensive – and it isn't just about sending someone on a course.

There are numerous ways people can develop their talents – sometimes it just involves thinking more creatively about what skills they need and how you can help them acquire or develop them. If employees see that you are prepared to put a bit of time and effort into helping them move forward, they are much more likely to be loyal, committed and prepared to put that little bit extra into the job they do for you.

Some of the ideas listed below may help to stimulate your thinking about how you can develop your employees.

→ **Short courses.** Short, sharp intensive programmes of study are often more manageable for a small business than lengthy taught qualifications. People are away from work for less time and the costs are usually more realistic. Find out what is on offer from your local college or specialist private providers.

→ **E-learning.** There are now many opportunities to acquire new skills via e-learning modules. It's a convenient, cost-effective way to develop your knowledge in bite-sized chunks at a time that suits you. A quick internet search should turn up e-learning courses that are relevant to your area.

→ **Job shadowing.** This can be a great way for employees to get a realistic view of what is involved in "the next step up" or to help them develop competency in a new area. You could consider letting one of your employees shadow you at sales pitches or presentations, for example, or on visits to potential new suppliers.

→ **Job swaps.** See if you can arrange a job swap for your employee with someone from another, non-competitive small business. You could even arrange for them to swap jobs for a short time with someone in one of your client companies – a great way for them to get a real insight into how your clients operate and what they need, while at the same time developing new skills.

→ **Mentoring.** Help your employee find a mentor who can help them think about how to approach situations at work, tackle areas they may be struggling with or identify ways of developing their skills. Some industries run formal mentoring schemes, but there's nothing to stop you setting up an informal arrangement in your own field if there are no existing programmes to draw on.

→ **Coaching.** Try taking a coaching approach to managing your employee. Help them think through work issues and share your experience of how best to tackle issues.

→ **Projects.** Giving an employee a specific project to manage is a great way of helping them develop competency in new areas. Make it a project that will stretch them, and support them by giving advice and guidance on how to tackle it.

→ **Skill-swap sessions.** Why not set up occasional lunch-time or breakfast sessions where members of the team take turns to share their knowledge and experience of a particular task or area? If you don't have enough people to do this internally, use your local professional networks to find other small businesses who might like to join you.

These are just a few ideas, which will hopefully give you some food for thought. Whichever method you choose, make sure you give your employees plenty of opportunity to apply what they have learned in your business. That way, everybody benefits!

 Checklist

☑ Put together a simple induction process that will help new recruits get up and running quickly.

☑ Plan for how you will support and manage your new recruit through their probationary period.

☑ Develop an appraisal system that will help you motivate and develop your employees.

☑ Keep the lines of communication open so that employees feel comfortable raising any issues or concerns between formal performance reviews.

☑ Think creatively about how you can develop the skills and talents of your employees.

A final word

I hope that this book has given you the confidence and competence to successfully take on your first few employees. It's worth investing the time and effort in getting the right systems in place from day one. That way you will be well prepared to take on even more new people and get them up and running rapidly as your business grows.

It's important to recognise, however, that over the course of time people will leave your business as well as join it. This may seem like a disaster at the time, particularly if it happens unexpectedly or at a very inconvenient time, but it is also an opportunity.

When someone departs for pastures new, it gives you the chance to take a hard look at the way work is being organised and to think about whether you could tackle and distribute tasks more effectively. What you needed in the early days may not necessarily be what you need as your business starts to expand and grow.

You may find that the nature of your work has changed, perhaps because of shifts in the markets you serve or because you have developed new products or services. General roles may need to become more specialised – or you may require new and different skill sets from your employees.

Jenny Smith of Harlowsave Credit Union says:

> Don't think that because someone has left you are going to find that person again. You won't ever replace like with like because everyone develops their job around their skills, abilities and their personality. When someone goes it gives you the chance to look at everyone's job description, assess whether you are using everyone's strengths to the full and decide if there needs to be a bit of a change around. If you can identify the gaps, it will help you work out what the job description and person specification for the new recruit should be.

Her view is endorsed by Karen Moule of Enterprise Marketing, who has been faced several times with the task of replacing employees for a variety of reasons, including relocation and the decision by an employee not to return after maternity leave. On each occasion, she has used her regular business coach to help her think through what kind of person she needed to recruit as a replacement and what the job description should be. As a result, she has taken on very different people, with different skill sets and levels of seniority each time. Karen stresses that this doesn't mean her original recruitment decisions were flawed. "They were all absolutely spot on for the stage I was at in the business at the time," she says.

Exit interviews

Make sure you don't miss the opportunity to get valuable feedback from people who do leave your business. An exit interview is a great way to capture vital knowledge you would like the departing employee to pass on – but it's also a good opportunity to get an honest picture of what it has been like working for your business.

Often people leave simply because their circumstances have changed, or they have been offered an opportunity they can't turn down. Sometimes, however, they have chosen to move on because they are unhappy in their role, have found the working atmosphere unpalatable or have experienced problems with a particular colleague. There are also times when people feel their contribution has not been recognised or that they have not been given the chance to develop their skills.

In an ideal world, you would have received warning signals about these issues early on and would have tried to respond to your employees' concerns. The reality of life in a small business, however, is that the sheer pressure of work often means that little niggles get overlooked – with the result that before too long, they turn into major issues which prompt a resignation.

Make sure you take the opportunity to get this kind of honest feedback from your employees before they depart, so that you can learn from it and avoid similar problems arising in the future.

Good luck with your recruitment – and may you find great people who will help your business thrive and grow.